I0789487

SHADOWING SARAH

A Psychosexual Novel

Irene Gillman, Ph.D. with Linda Pedreira

Copyright 2017 by Irene Gillman, Ph.D.

All rights reserved.

No part of this publication may be

reproduced or transmitted in any form or

by any means, electronic or mechanical, including photocopy,

recording, or any information storage and

retrieval system, without permission in

writing from the publisher.

ISBN: 1974438961
ISBN 13: 9781974438969

DEDICATION

To Moe, My First Tier Friend and Mentor

FOREWORD

Shadowing Sarah contains sexually explicit sections that may discomfort some readers; I am not one of them. As a long term therapist and teacher of human sexuality for over a decade, I recognize the value of pornography, with its main purpose being that of a conduit to sexual pleasure. On the other hand, the repression of sexual desires and fetishes engendered by guilty remorse is risky and harmful to the human psyche, as the primary character Sarah eventually comes to realize. Fantasies of this nature are not shameful, nor are exotic sexual acts to be deemed deviant since sex in any form is a healthy part of life for all creatures. The only caveat I offer regarding human sexual interaction is that it occurs between two consenting adults.

The title character in the book is indeed my shadow, just as much as I am hers and all of the others therapists I have known in my lifetime. She is not simply a conglomeration, but a fully realized heroine who took on a life of her own as the book progressed. I was sorry to say farewell to her once the last page was written.

I would be remiss if I did not speak about Linda Pedreira's contributions to the novel. She guided my characters along this journey, weaving their tales into a tapestry of touchstones for Sarah's evolution as well as my own. As such, Linda completed the pilgrimage I had started for Sarah, her patients, and myself.

In order to safeguard their privacy, I will not name the people that have given so much of themselves to me over the years - my family, friends, supervisors, students, patients, peers - as well as my own therapists - they know who they are and how much they all mean to me.

<u>A note about the text:</u> Italics are used to identify Sarah's inner thoughts and fantasies, which are featured throughout the book.

PROLOGUE

This is a tale of Sarah, a psychotherapist, and her patients who travel together on a journey of healing. Each of these eight patients seeks Sarah's guidance either in group and/or individual sessions. However, as they proceed on their odyssey, each revealing a different tale, Sarah becomes one with them as she ventures forth on her own internal quest towards mental salvation

First is **Stella the Sinner**, a woman whose relationships are torrid and rocky. She seeks control in all the wrong ways, but she stirs repressed emotions inside Sarah, which identifies them as fellow travelers, much to Sarah's consternation.

Second and third are **Barry and Gladys, the Married Couple**, depicted along with Sarah as the main characters in a three-act play. While the pair opens up about their innermost fantasies to Sarah and one another, Sarah immerses herself in her own complicated scenarios from the past.

Fourth is **Pauline the Lady-in-Waiting** who feels she is inadequate as a woman because she is unable to conceive or carry a child of her own. Sarah finds a kindred spirit in Pauline since she had been a pioneer in the early days of surrogacy. Further still, Pauline's plight revives strong emotions in Sarah that she believed had faded away long ago.

Fifth is **Catherine the Meddler** who expresses tremendous guilt over her constant interference in her son's family life, yet also believes she is justified in her actions. As she tries to reconcile Catherine's two opposing views, Sarah's self-confidence is startlingly shattered once again by the realization that she has not fully completed her original journey.

Sixth is **Paul the Knight-In-Arms** who pushes Sarah into familiar territory, one that she thought she had abandoned years ago. As her peer, Paul is a person of consequence for Sarah, but his persona not only opens up a part of her she believed to be long gone, but also propels her forward on her unfinished journey.

Seventh is **George the Fixer** who cannot control his calculating son, despite his desire to do so. His sorrow and anger grieve him and his tale of woe mirrors Sarah's early childhood. Yet, the question still haunts her: had she become a therapist to mend others' maladies or her own?

Eighth is **Hadassah the Wretch** who brings Sarah's dilemma into focus; as Hadassah's pain permeates Sarah's brain, she finally recognizes that she had not vanquished her inner demons at all. They were always there, lurking in the shadows just waiting for the right moment to strike. Sarah's moment of reckoning has come.

Last is **Sarah the Lost Pilgrim** who is forced to meet her doubts, her visions, her adversaries, her patients, and her hidden desires — all past and present — in a personal marathon that would test both her mettle and her endurance. During this race to the finish, Sarah is ultimately emboldened to behold her own image in the mirror of truth, only to discover once and for all that it is flawed.

Thus, as Sarah dutifully drives her patients towards their own self-revelations, which will ultimately point them onwards, Sarah loses her own way, haunted by disturbing images unwittingly conjured up by the unmasking of each of these travelers. Paradoxically, in helping her patients find their pathways, Sarah discovers that she herself has gone astray.

<u>Shadowing Sarah</u> depicts Sarah's dissolution that is the spark of her evolution. At the start, Sarah assumes she is healed completely, but her patients' memories forcefully yank her out of the shadows of illusion. In that way, each of them is indirectly rescuing her…a truth that becomes more evident as the sessions continue. Only when Sarah accepts her role as a fellow pilgrim is she able to guide herself and the others out of the shadowy layers that halt their progress towards the illuminating light of self-discovery.

Join them as they venture ahead…you just may find yourself somewhere along the way.

CHAPTER 1

OPENING THE DOOR

Sarah looked at the firmly shut door, studying its patterns of oaken wood as they swirled over the varnished veneer. As her eyes refocused on its somber solidity, her mind retraced the events of the past week, events that reminded her of the fragility of life with a startling clarity. Sarah's colleague had died suddenly and dramatically, taken by surprise, with no time to prepare. She grieved her loss… Diane with the brilliant mind and compassionate heart… and struggled to accept the undeniable certainty of Diane's being gone forever. Knowing that only direct action would help her get past her feelings of helplessness, Sarah had eagerly accepted the invitation to take on the role of leader for a therapy group that Diane had been conducting for the past eighteen months. Thus Sarah finds herself literally on the threshold of a new chapter, about to face the pilgrim souls on the other side of that door. She was anxious, yet thrilled at the same time. Would they accept her as Diane's replacement? Could she replace Diane in her own mind? Would Diane be lurking in the shadow somewhere, enviously stalking her usurper?

No, that's your own fear hoping to ambush you – Diane was a generous soul — always sharing and forever cheering me on.

At last, Sarah boldly pushed the door open to find a group of six men and women of different ages turning their faces towards her. In their eyes, she saw varying degrees of curiosity, sorrow, despair, suspicion, and, most of all, a sharp awareness of life's cruelties. Of course, Sarah had scrupulously reviewed Diane's notes, but she knew that she would have to devise her own interpretations going forward. She quickly made a mental note that one of the group was missing…had she been too angry or too hopeless to return to the sessions? Only time would tell.

Sarah had been systematically planning what she would try to accomplish in this initial session, which was to encourage them to face their feelings of loss, their grief, their anger, and their fears… she knew she would be touching on some raw nerves, but she felt she had to tear apart their wounds in order for the healing to begin. Yet, Sarah was overly anxious, realizing this would be the start of a crucial journey for her. Diane would shadow her, and that thought both comforted and disturbed her at the same time. She mentally threw back her shoulders, and entered the room.

As prepared as she was by her thorough review of Diane's therapy notes, Sarah was visibly startled by the first shout-out:

"Hello, I'm the gay one," uttered a stunning black man a bit nervously, yet in a jocular tone. *Was he trying to diffuse the tension, or vying for attention?* While not wanting to discourage his openness (and despite the fact that he was by far the best-looking person there), Sarah decided not to sacrifice the group for his sake, at least not at this juncture. After all, this was the first session of what she hoped would be a successful group experience for all of them right at the outset. If she were to permit one individual to dominate from the start, the outcome she needed to happen that first day would never materialize. So she glossed over his remark with a slight smile of acknowledgement, and turned her focus onto the group as a whole, who were all sitting in a protective circle, much like the covered wagons on the frontier that huddled together in that same formation when an attack was imminent. She began by introducing herself:

"Hello, my name is Sarah, your new group therapist. I am sorry for the loss of Diane, who was a close friend and dear to me as well. We all suffer losses and in this first meeting I would like us to discuss the loss as a group, and what it means to you all. But please first introduce yourself to me. I know you all know each other, but of course this is my initial session with you."

Sarah tensely waited for someone to speak first. She feared that she had silenced them all by refusing to accept that gamely gauntlet which had been thrown at her, half in jest and half in expectation. Had Diane run the group in that way, allowing each of them to have their turn while the rest listened in sympathy, apathy, or both? Sarah's familiar sense of foreboding, enhanced with a dash of vulnerability, was growing more intense by the second. *Say something… anything — tell me you're gay again – I'll pay attention to you this time!* As the silence grew longer and heavier with each passing moment, Sarah went from one face to another, searching for some type of response.

My God – what a great beginning this is! Why did I ever think I could pick up where Diane left off without even missing a beat? I could hear my mother's voice hissing into my brain: you think you're so smart, don't you? I always warned you that you were way too sure of yourself. Remember where you come from, young lady! You're no better than me…Oh please, somebody up there, help me find my way again…

Sarah inwardly groaned; her confidence was fading fast. Then - out of nowhere — an answer to her silent prayer…her mother's taunts were being drowned out by a very pretty younger woman with a sweet countenance. She rose from her chair, looked around at the others as if chiding them, and spoke in a voice that was as lovely as she was:

"My name is Pauline. I am married, but have no children, not by choice, but because I have been unable to conceive a baby…but not through lack of trying!"

Sarah heard a few suppressed titters at Pauline's last remark and could not help but wonder:

Had she consciously made a joke to lighten the mood? Whether it was deliberately or subconsciously done, I am deeply thankful to her.

Embarrassed by the group's reaction, Pauline continues her narrative in a much lower voice than before:

"Instead of adoption, my husband prefers surrogacy, but I can't help worrying about the future. I fear how strangers may make comments on how the child so strongly resembles my husband, and I know that as the child gets older, nagging questions will come up. I am in this group to decide if surrogacy is the right choice for me. The fact will always remain that I am not the biological mother. I understand and have come to accept that reality. Just as any other adoptive parent, I will have difficulties knowing when and how to tell my child about its background, but this is more of a special case, don't you think? I suppose that my husband and I will have to figure out how to explain that I am the "real" mother when the time comes. Our prior therapist was very helpful to me and I am not sure how this will go with you as the new therapist. She understood my situation, but I am willing to give you a chance."

Sarah gave thanks for her tale; she felt fairly certain she could be a helpful guide to this new patient since she had experienced what Pauline was going through first-hand, but now was not the time or the place to reveal this history to her. Instead, Sarah hastened to reassure her by saying,

"I understand how hard it is to share anything personal with someone new. So please feel free to only talk about what you are comfortable sharing. Anyone else care to tell me why you are here?"

A well-dressed distinguished gentleman in his early forties spoke in a subdued and quiet voice as if he were ashamed of his tale, even though he had most likely shared it with Diane and the group before. However, Sarah knew the first time was always the most difficult so she presented him with her most sympathetic face. He looked around the room and began:

"I'm Barry. My wife Gladys, who is not a member of this group, and I are having great difficulties in our marriage. We fight all the time about who's right and who's wrong and we have lots of trouble in the bedroom. What I've gotten out of this group under Diane's guidance is some understanding of what our conflicts are about. Gladys is always trying to be the boss of me. What I'm finding helpful in this group is that I can see other people trying to control or influence others in the group…and that helps me see what I'm doing and what my wife is doing without being in the midst of an over-emotional interaction with her."

Barry had given Sarah an important insight into the group dynamics. Perhaps her initial hunch about Diane's methodology had been correct. Sarah decided it would be best to follow her friend's lead for a while until she had her sea legs. Another of the group quickly followed — this time a man in his fifties — who had an open and direct look about him. He spoke strongly, as if he was used to telling this tale, but he kept his gaze on the floor, most likely because he was embarrassed to directly face Sarah, who was a newcomer to their circle.

"My name's George. I'm the parent of a son who is addicted to heroin. I don't even have to go into the excruciating details about the trouble I have in dealing with this issue. Everyone here has heard about it ad nauseam. The situation is killing me and my family. I am always in conflict about whether I am either helping my son or enabling him. I love him and want him to be OK. Anyone who has a child with some kind of disability knows what I'm talking about and people in this group have been very helpful to me about making decisions in a wise way — not just giving, giving, giving to my kid. I've been told my kid is a 'User.' (He said the word as if that was his son's actual name.) Some might call him a sociopath, but I think that's too strong a word. He doesn't commit outright crimes, but he manipulates everyone to get what he wants from them, which is usually more money to feed his awful habit. He doesn't seem like a feeling or caring person — so I am terribly disappointed in him. Diane was dealing with this by getting me to see how others in this group sometimes manipulate or are manipulated by people close to them. Once I learn how to read him better, then I will be able to more easily recognize the signs that indicate when my son is using me or someone else in the family. But I still need help!"

Sarah could feel George's sense of loss more deeply than the previous group members who had spoken up. He had been set adrift, abandoned, and was on a path to despair. Sarah knew that journey all too well, but could not allow herself to dwell on the past now…not unless it made her more empathetic here. Like Barry, George had given Sarah further clues as to what Diane was doing here…what George was referring to when he spoke about Diane's guidance is what is known in the field of psychology as "mentalization." He spoke a good game, using terms straight out of Psych 101, but he could truly visualize neither his own — nor his son's feelings and motivations, at least not at the present time… but Sarah planned on changing that perspective in the future.

At this point, Sarah wanted to refocus on the rest of the group, and so she directly addressed the remaining members who had not yet spoken, including the self-described gay man who had been so eager to share at the beginning of the session. She ardently *(I am drawn to him sexually…I can feel his passion inside me…)* hoped she had not shut him down completely, and tried reaching him:

"So far everyone has been quite open. Is there some reason that you are not volunteering to speak?" Although Sarah was looking directly at him, an older woman who had seemed disinterested and uninvolved shook things up by opening her mouth, but not introducing herself:

"I find it hard to talk about my issues to a stranger and you are a stranger."

While her bluntness was stinging, Sarah jumped at the un-expected opportunity this woman had unknowingly given her, which was the perfect lead-in to the overdue introduction. Sarah had intended to do that part much earlier (it was number one on her carefully organized agenda), but delayed because she had not wanted to stop the ebb-and-flow of the earlier dialogues. Feeling braver now, Sarah launched into her own unfinished tale:

"I have already given you my name, but not much more. It may take some time to get to know me, but I will share some prelimi-nary facts about me. It might make it easier for you to get used to me and my style. Every therapist has a different way of being a therapist — so I do understand how tough it is to accept a new one without knowing my approach. So here goes — then maybe you will feel more comfortable."

After her brief speech, the group looked at Sarah with more curiosity than suspicious anxiety now. Seeing the change in their mannerisms towards her, Sarah felt comfortable enough to continue:

"I have been a therapist for many years and I have also been in therapy about half my life. You should know that everyone has problems-including therapists. I have been divorced twice, and have two kids with whom I have had difficulties, much like some of you who are parents. We all have relationship issues, and as such, we all have to learn how to know ourselves and understand oth-ers from their perspective. Before we start therapy, we often think that we have to fix the other people in our lives, but in reality it's ourselves that we have to fix and/or change. So my goal as your therapist is to have the type of relationship with you that shows you how to change yourself by seeing how you interact with others in the group as well as with me. That's why I believe it is important for all of you to not only be in this group on a regular basis, but also to have individual sessions with me so that we can establish a bond of trust. We need to differentiate between our 'persona,' which is what we show to others both inside and outside of this group, and who we truly are inside-our 'inner self'-which is what you will share with me if we make the right connection. I'm not saying it will be simple; it will take time and effort."

Sarah had rehearsed that monologue several times, hoping that this simple, yet introspective history as well as her openness would give them a bit of comfort. She was immediately gratified when the reluctant woman spoke again, this time with more warmth:

"Ok thanks. You have made me feel more comfortable. I am very embarrassed about some of my relationships, especially the one I have with my daughter-in-law. She and I are always at each other. We fight over anything and actually call each other names. It's pretty awful and I am ashamed of my shortcomings with her. The others have all heard about our conflicts — sometimes word for word — and I feel as if I am being suffocated by the appalling ugliness of the situation. When I am with her, she changes me into someone I don't recognize — and certainly do not want to be!"

Turning to Sarah, she apologetically added this afterthought,

"By the way, my name is Catherine."

Her willingness prodded the others — the recalcitrant gay man finally spoke up:

"I am Paul, also known as 'The Gay One.' Well, you all know how I am struggling with being gay. I guess that's why I made that stupid remark earlier. I was once married to a woman and have a child, but now I am considering marrying my male partner. And what do you think concerns my possible future in-laws? Can we have a kid…and then how do we deal with the kid in terms of having two male parents? It's very tricky."

As an aside, he turned to Sarah and in a coy way confided,

"By the way, I'm also a licensed psychologist so we have much in common here."

Sarah addressed him fervently *(Sarah, don't lean in so close to him-control your desire for once in your life!)*, trying to make him feel more comfortable so that he would be willing to continue in this same vein in future sessions. She felt that she could help him, now that she had been given a glimpse into his sexual confusion. Speaking in a deep voice that she knew to be her sexiest (she just couldn't resist), Sarah answered him:

"Paul, I am happy that you were able to talk about this in front of me and the group. I was always a rebel-acting out against being a female in the old days when women really could not be as free as males. I ached to be one of the boys. Please understand that I did not want a penis *(I wonder how large Paul's is…I tried to picture it in my mind)* and most definitely did not have "penis envy" à la Freud, but there was always confusion about one's sexual proclivity-especially as an adolescent. Girls, and I include myself here, often have crushes on other girls. In the same way, boys play games by showing off their penises to other boys. I believe we are all born bisexuals and go in one direction or the other — or sometimes remain in the middle. It must have been rough on you growing up and struggling with this issue."

Sarah continued in this same vein:

"My first patient was gay and just like you started off by saying he was gay. I questioned him as to why he had started our first meeting with that introduction – not his name, but his sexual preference. I gently remonstrated with him that heterosexuals don't come in saying they are heterosexual and we went from there. As we continued our sessions, he became physically attracted to me. It's known as transference in psychoanalytic therapy.—"

Now why did I have to tell him about that? Am I wishing for something like that to happen with him? Sarah, what's happening to you? Here my mother comes again, that venomous voice reminding me that I was no better than a common whore!

Swatting away that last incessant buzzing in her ears, Sarah clarified further:

"He had also been married — you would be astounded by the frequency of such unions — and had a daughter. He now was acknowledging to the world that he preferred males, not just in bed but in a loving relationship. So I do understand your dilemma."

Paul's look remained slightly flirtatious, but it was more conspiratorial now instead of cocky. Sarah longed to engage him further, but firmly reverted back to reality. She noticed that there was one woman who had sat silently through the session so far. Sarah wanted to reach her before the session ended so she addressed her directly by asking,

"And what about you?"

The woman appeared to be too much in anguish to speak. Her eyes were red-rimmed and teary-she was obviously upset with the new changes in the group, but did not appear past remedy. Sarah clung to her professional, if rushed observation as the woman started to speak in a quiet, almost hushed tone:

"My name is Hadassah…no mistaking my background. I am the daughter of Jewish survivors of Nazi Germany. My parents came here as children-somehow they made it through and met here in a synagogue as adults. Despite their relatively good fortune, they were always depressed and unhappy and passed that heaviness on to me. I never feel like I can be happy — perhaps because they made me feel that I do not deserve to have joy in my life in the same way that they could not relish their being alive. I always feel that same burden of guilt and could never find a man to lift me out of my fate. I'm seventy and still alone. Now that Diane has also left me, I feel more abandoned and hopeless than before, if that's even possible!"

Sarah could inherently feel Hadassah's sorrow deep within her marrow. Her wretchedness was so palpable that it infiltrated the room and all of its inhabitants. Sarah resolved to withstand it by providing her with a clinical analysis,

"I'm sure you know that is called survivor guilt."

Hadassah muffled a deep sob — an outward sign of her immense disappointment and dismay at Sarah's simplistic diagnosis. She lifted her eyes to meet Sarah's, hoping to find just a tiny bit of sympathy in her.

But instead of reaching out to this soul who was so obviously in agony, Sarah brusquely brushed her aside.

I have to lift the mood in this room. She is really making me anxious. I guess I'll have to deal with her at some point — just not now! I don't know why, but this one scares me – I think she reminds me of a recurring nightmare I had as a child — a vengeful ogress or something like that.

She had to grab the moment as she saw it… her therapist's instincts had told her that Hadassah's pulsating grief would be the perfect segue into her main purpose here, which was to get them to first describe, then share, and finally accept their loss of Diane. Without that, Sarah believed she would not be able to make the progress she needed in this first meeting. So, taking advantage of the opening that Hadassah had unintentionally given her, Sarah was able to return to her original step-by-step strategy by first asking them to start talking about their feelings on losing Diane. She was pleased to hear Catherine speak first, since she had been openly defiant about sharing her feelings with Sarah, Diane's replacement:

"About the loss of Diane… I miss her terribly. Her death was unexpected and set off strong feelings of depression in me. I can barely get out of bed in the morning-I feel so lost and even betrayed, first by Diane, and then by God or destiny. It all seems so unfair — to take her away from all of us now, when we were finally coming together as a group. I feel selfish about these feelings, but can't help it. Is anyone else suffering? Or is this just my own inability to deal with loss?"

Barry spoke almost diffidently:

"Diane was OK. She tried her best to help Gladys and me, but to be honest, we were not making any real progress. Gladys wanted to quit altogether…not too surprising since she never wanted to be in therapy in the first place. I was becoming a bit frustrated myself so I was going to inform Diane that we wanted to take a breather, but then she died. I'm glad I didn't have to have that conversation with her. I hated to let her down…"

Barry looked sheepishly around the room to see if anyone else had the same relieved reaction, but no one met his eyes. Sarah felt sorry for him — she knew he was a little ashamed of what he had just said — and she was about to say something helpful, but then George spoke up:

"Gee Barry, I could see someone else — and you all know who I mean here — the missing-in-action person — being so selfish, but not you! I am just broken up by the whole lousy experience. Diane was a true friend…she spoke her mind, never afraid to call me out on what I was doing wrong with my son. Sure, she made me angry sometimes — especially when she put the blame on me for my son's behavior, but she was probably right. I am stuck now – Diane's gone and her work is incomplete. I feel abandoned too…I suppose that's the best word to describe my feelings."

Pauline had been taking in everything that was said. She looked deep in thought and hesitated twice before finally speaking:

"I suppose my reaction to Diane's death is a little bit of every-thing that was already said by the others. I certainly have a sense of abandonment like George because Diane was going to help me make a difficult decision, but we had only just begun to discuss it. So, I feel betrayed by fate, much like Catherine, but at the same time, I am relieved like Barry because I did not get the sense that Diane could really relate to my situation. I dreaded disappointing her and myself. Now I am anxious to start the process anew with you Sarah."

Sarah was ecstatic when she heard this last revelation.

I think I can…I think I can…I think I can…that refrain from the story about "the little engine that could." I used to read that story aloud to both of my children at bedtime every night. Pauline is my catalyst. She is strong enough to bring the group together — they will follow her lead, I am sure of it.

Paul seconded Pauline's thoughts, even more forcefully than she had done:

"Sarah, I think you're just what the doctor ordered — for all of us. Yes, we are sorry about Diane, but we need you to finish what she started. I'm not ready to let the last eighteen months just self-destruct. C'mon, all of us have worked so hard. Let's give the new girl in town a chance!"

This man is my knight in shining armor alright! My enthusiasm for this project is growing. I can work with these people. Diane, I promise I will not let you down.

After almost everyone had shared their feelings, Sarah was convinced they had begun a new and important journey together. For some reason, much like the rest of the group, she either did not notice or chose to ignore Hadassah sitting quietly in her chair. Her eyes were simmering, but she hid them so well, as if this was a talent she had painstakingly fostered over the years. She just seemed to melt into the background, seeking out a crumb of attention for one second, and then scuttling back into her invisibility for another. Perhaps if Sarah had even slightly noticed these almost imperceptible mood shifts, Hadassah may have ventured along with the rest...but that was not to be, at least not for today.

Just before everyone left though, Sarah did turn her attention towards the one person who was missing – Stella. Sarah asked about her, and again it was Catherine who spoke first:

"Oh, Stella isn't here tonight. She had another event she had to go to with her husband. She is dealing with abuse issues, but when she's back she can share that with you."

Do I detect an ulterior motive here? Catherine could be devious...

Sarah winced at the betrayal and invasion of Stella's privacy. While this was a group used to sharing their experiences and thoughts with one another, Sarah could not help but feel as if someone had divulged a page out of a secret journal to her...the thumbnail sketch made her uncomfortable and she decided to meet Stella in an individual session, if possible, before exposing her to the group's scrutiny in front of a strange therapist. If not, Stella might decide to run for the hills...

Sarah shook off the thought, wished all six of them a good week, and promised to arrange individual sessions with them before their next meeting. The door had been opened and it was her strong intention to leave it ajar so that her soon-to-be kindred spirits could continue on their pilgrimages freely, with Sarah as their intrepid guide.

CHAPTER 2

STELLA THE SINNER

Something in Stella's voice in that first phone conversation made Sarah uncomfortable, yet eager to meet her, especially after hearing about her in the group session. She spoke with a low tremor that was hesitant, even though the conversation concerned banalities for the most part…scheduling an appointment to meet at a convenient time, directions to the office, how to cancel if necessary, etc. No, there was nothing unusual in what she said, yet her manner and tone struck a chord within Sarah: it was not a long-lost lullaby, or an old lover's serenade, or the soundtrack to a favorite film (unless it was a horror movie). It was just that she sounded eerily familiar — an echo of someone Sarah had once known, but not really-

Why should Sarah, a psychotherapist who has treated patients, taught at universities, trained other psychologists, and published articles for scientific journals over several decades, feel such trepidation? New patients always usher in a new set of feelings: anxiety over which course of treatment might fit best, optimism when things go smoothly, sorrow over what might be revealed in the sessions, and faith in the healing process. Stella would encompass all these possible reactions, but there was something else that bespoke caution. And so it was that when the time for that first meeting arrived, Sarah dreaded what she would find in the woman whose voice conjured up old ghosts and bugaboos. She had felt some tension immediately before that first group meeting, but that was only natural, while this was something else entirely — a warning perhaps. Who would be sitting in the waiting room? Stella? Sarah's mother? An ex-husband? Herself?

Stella is sitting quietly in the shadows, partially hidden on a metal stool that a receptionist had placed in an alcove. No one chose that seat, simply because often it was not available. Files, envelopes, or other office paraphernalia usually slumped there haphazardly until they either fell in a heap upon the floor or were delegated to another room. That is probably what happened and so Stella had taken advantage of a secure hiding place, but why? Was it a hint to the mystery I was trying to solve or was it that she wanted me to seek her out from the get-go? I do not play games with my patients; I prefer a more direct intervention, yet Stella called to me, cajoling me to follow her in a different way. Had someone in the group told Stella something about me — some unknown quirk that I was unaware of? The thought threw me off a bit, but nevertheless, I was determined to persevere.

I strode over to her secret perch, and as I did so, she blinked at me. It was more like a sly wink, flirtatiously bold, daring me to meet her challenge. Yet, at the same time, her posture was bent like that of a supplicant praying at an altar. She was a vamp that made her modesty appear off-color…and that was just my first impression. She looked me over in a child-like way, much like my daughter did on her first day at school. Did Stella's voice remind me of my daughter? I shook off the thought, but it had unsettled me. Where was my signature self-confidence? Where would Stella lead me and did I really want to go there?

Once inside the office, Sarah took her customary seat and felt more like "Charles in Charge" again — in control and eager to help her patient. Stella's stance had modified itself; she sat facing Sarah, her face open and innocent, in contrast to her age, which

Sarah judged to be mid-forties. She had clearly planned out her outfit for days. Her accessories all matched: dark green stones decorated her throat, wrists, and ears, while her body was encased in earth tones ("encased" because her dress was one size too small and Sarah wondered if that was deliberate or simply because of a recent weight gain. She made a mental note to ask her about that once they had developed a comfort level that suited them both). Her make-up was too dark for her light skin, but it dramatized her hazel eyes, which would have been lost due to their narrowness. They appeared to shrink within her forehead, peeping out at Sarah from another hiding place — almost like a cobra, yet not as sinister. Her beige-colored hair was streaked with fresh highlights. Was this a new look for her, a fresh start that would eradicate her past? Sarah found herself attracted to Stella – she gave off a strong sexual vibe that she was well aware of - and probably used often to give her a sense of control. Sarah was eager to learn more, but intuitively knew what Stella would reveal.

I waited for her to speak first. It took some time before she was able to find the words she needed to say. In that interval, images flooded into my mind, images that I had believed were vanquished forever through years of therapy and self-discovery. The memories were crystal-clear so that when Stella began, her words came as no surprise.

"I was sexually abused by my grandfather. It started when I was five years old."

A figure burst into my brain, startling in its clarity: my Uncle Frank whispering in my ear as I tried to sleep, hoping he would leave as silently as he had entered. What was he saying? I struggled to not hear him. I thought I had buried him, but here he was, unexpected and unwelcome. I turned to Stella, with his breath still warmly moist and putrid upon my face, as she continued her confession.

"I was the one who made it happen. I flirted with him shamelessly because I wanted to test my sexiness. I suppose you could say that I wanted to turn him on."

Having boldly flung off her shoes when she first settled into the chair opposite Sarah, Stella wriggled her freshly pedicured toes, complete with sunflower decals that were in sharp contrast to the rest of her, and pointed them at Sarah, as if daring her to be shocked by what she had said. Fighting off the "Aha!" scream rising within her, only because she heard her inner thoughts expressed by this stranger, Sarah nonchalantly inquired,

"At the age of five?"

I tried to remember when my own nights with Uncle Frank started. Was I only five? No, I couldn't have been that young...I pushed his specter away forcefully, as I should have done so long ago. No! What happened was not my fault...hadn't I been through all of that in therapy? What was it about this new patient that made me start that old blame-game again? Blame – punishment — father — mother — and me... an all-too-familiar vortex spinning in my brain.

My father stood before me now, grinning widely as he sometimes did. Of course, I always favored him over my mother who was so cold and demanding. Never praising me, never believing in me, never showing any affection at all...whereas my father, though stern and sometimes physically abusive when pushed to the boiling point, was always more caring. Had I somehow encouraged his beatings? Was I trying to punish my mother by taking his attention away from her? I thought I had solved my family dynamics long ago so why was this unwelcome interrogation hammering its way into my psyche?

Stella turned her attention firmly back to Stella.

Every time I say that name, I hear Brando's Stanley bellowing like a wounded beast...for God's sake, control yourself! Listen to her.

"No, not that young...it probably started when I was around 11 or so."

Sarah heard her disembodied voice challenging Stella, "Did part of you enjoy what was happening to you?"

I knew I should never have said that, not this early into therapy. What made me ask it — my own unmerited feelings of shame...or my wanting to push Stella into a catalytic confrontation?

Stella hesitated, visibly turning the question around, tossing it this way and that, then catching it with that sly smile.

What a vixen she is…but her charms are irresistible. Her lips look so supple — how do they taste — how do they kiss — how do they lick? Her allure is overpowering. I know she knows I want to pull her out of her seat towards me. Our bodies would be so soft against one another, like down pillows. This could be a new and delightful experience for both of us, instead of the harsh love-making we oftentimes both had to endure from the time we reached pre-pubescence…

Forcing herself to stop this most inappropriate daydream, Sarah watched her patient's facial expressions shift from incredulity to disgust to outrage. She appeared to be arguing with herself, duplicating Sarah's own inner confrontation with herself moments before. Sarah first thought that Stella's internal struggle concerned her giving in to this unexpected impulse. She was obviously in the middle of a crisis, which was not uncommon with first therapy sessions. Sarah empathized with her struggles, but showed no outward sympathy. Then, without warning, Stella turned on Sarah. She should have been expecting the rage, been prepared to counter the accusations, the threats, the insults…the sheer meltdown, but had been waylaid by her own secret longing. Sarah opened her mouth to speak, but-

My memories insist on interrupting me. I recall brutal beatings for small infractions. My father seemed to enjoy spanking me…he would draw the punishment out by first taking me firmly by the hand to lead me into his study. Then he would close the door and lock it, making sure I would hear the click. (The sound of a lock clicking still makes me sweat, like Pavlov's dogs.) He would make me remove my underwear, but not my skirt and draw me slowly across his knees. Then he would lift my skirt and wait for 30 seconds. I think the agony of that brief interval was worse than the actual spanking. He would breathe deeply and then begin, his bare hand striking my backside slowly at first and then quickening. He would never draw blood, but my skin turned dark red, like the claret he would enjoy afterwards as he watched me put on my underwear again. The ritual included looking at my backside in a small mirror, which he would hand me so that I could see the physical changes he had wrought upon me. He wanted me to see the red mark as a kind of Scarlet Letter-a symbol of shame, but I viewed it as a badge of honor. His control over me was infinite and complete.

After a while, it became a weekly routine. I would misbehave, then I would be spanked, and afterwards my father would bring home a toy or a book for me as a present for my good behavior. I felt empowered then, but soon I would misbehave and the power would shift back to him. Was I misbehaving because I actually enjoyed the spankings and their aftermath? Were those brief moments of control an aphrodisiac even in a child so young? Did I realize that this pattern would so drastically trace out my life?

Sarah awoke from her self-induced trance. Before her stood Stella, her face still contorted, but her eyes staring at Sarah with silent recognition. Did she see in Sarah a fellow traveler? Her fury subsided into a shared understanding. She looked relieved, yet not altogether innocent, and her glance was all-knowing.

Had she somehow sensed my flashback or even worse, my fantasy about her?

"No, Sarah dear - I never enjoyed any part of it. Grandpapa was the one who came at me first, with no encouragement at all. I just bore it until it ended when I turned seventeen. I guess he preferred his girls to be younger."

"But what about afterwards? There had to have been consequences, or you would not be seeking my help."

"I don't want to blame all of my problems on my childhood. I think that's the coward's way out. No, I want to be able to accept the blame for my failures — myself, no one else! I even go so far as to fake orgasms just to get it over with — just to please my partner so I won't have to keep putting up with all the useless gyrations...

do you ever do that? All women do at one time or another, don't we?"

Sarah felt more ill-at-ease than ever. Had this woman somehow got a glimpse of her soul? Who was the therapist in the room?

My life is rewinding, going back twenty years in the blink of an eye — back to my sex therapist…Walter - he seemed especially interested in my sexual inadequacies. I had just admitted that I was in the habit of faking orgasms to satisfy my lovers…my childhood abuses had sullied sex for me. Walter explained that this was a natural reaction — being afraid to fully experience my own sexuality after having been abused. At the next session, he gave me a gift — a white dildo that he taught me to use. He placed my legs apart on his corduroy couch – I can still feel its rough ripples hugging my lower naked body — and took off my panties. Strangely enough, he did not remove my skirt, just like my father. He inserted the device into me very cautiously and showed me how to work it. I came pretty quickly, averting my face away from Walter as he intensely watched my movements. I took it home to experiment further, but I preferred to use it with Walter present. I knew I was exciting him and I absolutely reveled in this new-found control!

Sarah decided to share some of these insights with Stella;

"I see it from a different angle. Your childhood abuse makes you ill at ease with your own sexuality so you do not believe you deserve an orgasm. You know that to be the case since you would not have mentioned those incidents if you did not believe that they caused considerable damage. In fact, that was the first sentence out of your mouth. Can you not see the significance?"

Once again, that coy smile and flirtatious eyes flickered across her face and lingered for a while, almost as if they were in on a secret joke. She was teasing Sarah just like she did before. This was not what Sarah wanted or expected to happen. Her own ghosts had to be vanquished before she could help Stella defeat her own. As Sarah spoke to her, her voice rang out clearly; she was speaking to both of them at that point.

"You blame yourself and take the subsequent punishment for what you believe are your sins, but that is not what happened here. You prefer sinfulness over powerlessness. By imagining that you were in control of the abuse that occurred, you thought you were also at fault. But that is not the case. You were the victim of abuse and that will not change until you change your perception of what happened."

I was startled to hear what had just come out of my mouth. I understood the truth of my statement intellectually, but I recognized that I had never truly felt it in my heart. That is why Stella's experiences so reverberated within me; her defensive denials echoed my own. She succeeded in uprooting my secret garden that I thought had been so neatly re-planted by my therapy. Here was a second revelation…a rebirth, so to speak, of another me so late in life!

Changing such childhood perceptions and behavior is more difficult than Sarah had blithely imagined. She had more roads to travel with Stella, as her shadowy memories poked a glaring searchlight onto hers. It was uncanny how their so-seemingly different lives wove together in what can only be called a "crazy-quilt."

In the next sessions, Stella described her marriages, one past and one current. She wanted so desperately not to repeat the patterns, but as each relationship was examined, she saw that she had participated with both of her husbands in the same old flawed dynamic: abuser — victim, victim — abuser, controller — controlee, power vs. submission. She and her husband both took part in splitting off parts of themselves, each taking turns as the Controller. Her first marriage was a violent rematch of her prior relationships. When she was the victim, and he the abuser, she was able to regain power because he regretted his actions and would buy her small gifts to compensate for his actions. After a while though, he would become angry at her. Then the pattern would begin again and continue because they were both unaware of their own contributions to the cycle.

This husband was not her first love, but he was definitely her first passion. They experimented with sadomasochistic role-playing until he carried it too far. When she was pregnant, he insisted on continuing to spank her mercilessly. He was unable to enjoy sex without this violent foreplay, something that never appealed to Stella. She was no masochist; she only wanted to please her partners.

"He liked to see my skin welt up and hear my screams. I suppose he thought I enjoyed it too. After a while, though, I tried to put the brakes on, especially in my eighth month…he just wouldn't stop. Pretty soon, he started to beat me outside of the bedroom. He stopped for a while after the baby was born. He went around like a proud papa — his son was all he could talk about!"

"Then, what happened?"

Her answer was not unexpected, but jarring nonetheless…

"I began to punish the boy — just to get back at him. When our son turned three, the sexual violence escalated…no more naughty spankings, not even hard slaps across my backside and face. Sometimes he punched me — hard! Other times, he used his belt along with his fists. So, I turned on the child. First, it was just coldness on my part — no goodnight kisses or hugs. Then I began whacking him if he spilled something or looked at me in the wrong way."

"Did you feel vindicated?"

"Not really. He was my rival. He was taking the attention away from me. By punishing him, I thought I was in control behind my husband's back, but I never was — not really. One day, I just walked out. I left no note, just a chicken defrosting in the sink. I wonder if they ever ate it. Funny, I just remembered that…the blood oozing out of its white bumpy flesh dripping into the sink. Do you think there's some symbolism there?"

I had to smile, but then my own memories landed hard, like her husband's punch. My first husband was also abusive towards me, but I was used to that kind of relationship, from my uncle's sexual abuse and my father's physical punishments. But, in my first marriage, the roles of abuser and victim were also reversed. We had no children at the time, so he and I role-played, with me as the mother (the boss) and he as the child (the submissive one), and then vice-versa. At first, it was tender and harmless, almost cute in a way. It was our hidden world, never to be shared with outsiders. I would speak baby-talk to him and he would caress me as a child would. I loved that time of my life, never paying attention to the warning signs that sounded in my head, as loudly as a smoke alarm.

First, he threw a few belittling comments, just to test the waters. His tone was jocular, then incredulous, then sarcastic: "You are just adorable when you can't find your car keys…You must be kidding – Maybe you need to take a smart pill along with those vitamins…" He was continually eroding my self-esteem with biting insults, first in private and then in public — our "Universe of Two" was no more. After a particularly bruising public display in front of our peers, he brought me a bouquet of tulips "for no reason except that I love and cherish you." I licked my wounds and forced myself to believe him — for far too long. Like Stella and her partners, we allowed and even wanted the cycle to continue because we enjoyed it when we regained power and we hoped the pattern would end, but of course, it never did.

Then the conflicts turned physical — first a slap, then another, and then full-blown beatings — always behind closed doors. He would force me to give in to him sexually and I would do it because I was afraid of what would happen if I didn't do what he wanted. I succumbed to his wishes, often kneeling before him as he probed my anus with his thick fingers. His physicality was staggering and his demands limitless. He wanted to fill every opening in my body so that I would lie helpless before him. He even bought handcuffs and a blindfold, which I found quite erotic. It was the age-old paradox — letting go of control gives you more power…and more pleasure.

At one point, I was back on top…at least in the world outside of my home. I had earned my PhD, began teaching at a local university, started a private practice, and even ran a clinic for battered women. How ironic and sad that at the time I was unable to identify with my patients as one of their own...I was so blind! Eventually, my husband regained even more control by hurling unspeakable invectives at me in front of everyone, and subduing me with his belt even in front of our daughter. I would seek revenge by punishing her in the same love-withheld-way until a pattern had been rigidly established, a pattern that was nearly impossible to alter...until I walked away, much like Stella had done. No, I did not leave a defrosting chicken for their dinner. I don't think I wanted to imagine them both sitting down to dinner afterwards — my heart was too broken to plan even one last supper. Leaving the people you love so deeply shakes your inner core. I never thought I would recover, and question my decision relentlessly, even after understanding why I had to do it, even to this day.

When I met my second husband, who was younger than me, I was a stronger person, but I was still licking the scars left from my first marriage. Determined not to repeat the same mistakes (as many people who had endured an abusive relationship do), I married a gentle man who was both caring and passionate. As someone who was older, I was sure I would take the lead in that partnership. Yet, many of the old habits returned, but in different ways. To begin with, the age difference made me susceptible to jealousy. He was physically attractive and an outrageous flirt; at first, I tried ignoring this behavior, but gradually grew irritated, anxious and angry at the way he made me feel. This was abuse; it started with him hurting my feelings but it contributed to my own self-destructive inclinations: I blamed my angry feelings on myself, then him, which only led to more confrontations between us. We fought over the way he paid too much attention to my sexy friend. His frustration bubbled over into silly acts of vengeance, like throwing my clothing out of the window. The cycle had begun again, and even though I was very aware of what was happening here, I was unable to disengage myself from the past. The damage was already done and I again felt responsible for what had happened to us; guilt — guilt — guilt!

Sarah then glanced over at Stella, who appeared to be ready for battle! Sarah was not surprised since this reverie was a long one that had diverted her attention away from Stella's discussion of her second marriage. Like many seekers of a more perfect union, Stella wanted a fresh start, but if you do not face the realities and the dynamics of what went wrong in your childhood or love relationships, you will never be able to avoid the same pitfalls. She was enraged that her second marriage had turned out to be a repeat of the first. She looked at Sarah, not just for sympathy, but empathy.

"Why does this keep happening to me," she screamed in a squeal that bespoke her pain. "I am not to blame here. He thinks I like being beaten…no one does! When I beg him to stop, he just turns it up more. Look at these bruises!"

She pulled up the sleeves of her neutral-toned long-sleeved dress to uncover a series of angry marks in varying shades of dark eggplant and even deeper cobalt-green shades — a vivid testament to her ordeals. She wanted Sarah to feel sorry for her, even to identify with her - Sarah forced herself not to react. She knew it was too soon to explain to her that fighting was a way for couples to connect on an emotional level…that aggression often led to apology, intimacy, and sometimes sexual arousal. Since Stella and her husband were now only able to connect through physical assault or sex, their arguments served as foreplay to what is literally defined as "make-up sex."

"What brings on these assaults? Give me a typical scenario," Sarah calmly instructed her.

Stella's reaction was fierce and immediate:

"What kind of therapist are you??? No, what kind of woman are you??? Are you blaming me??? You know — you sound just like my mother…she was just so controlling, always insisting that she was right and I was wrong! All we did was fight — she taking the other person's side and telling me whatever went wrong was all my fault… and me exploding at her, anger just gushing out of me…scalding and bitter. I knew she would never believe me if I told her about anything — my perverted grandfather or my vicious husband — so I just raged at her. Our relationship was based on conflict — day in and day out. I can't remember ever having a quiet conversation with her. All she did was pick-pick-pick at me until I practically clawed at her with my words. Now, here I am, coming to you for help and you have her same aggravating attitude, so I want to hear what you really think about me because I'm more than ready to tell you my opinion about you and… P.S., it's not too flattering!"

Her tone was accusatory and challenging. It was obvious to Sarah that Stella wanted to incite her into an argument because she was more comfortable in an adversarial position; it was how she usually interacted with most of the significant people in her life, but Sarah refused to allow Stella to embrace the repetitious behavior that had become a type of security blanket for her. Patients will wish to repeat the same negative, yet reassuring pattern within the therapeutic relationship; by not allowing Stella to continue this destructive routine, Sarah was focused on leading Stella into a total understanding of her behavior, which was that she was following a flawed template. Once she learned that important fact, she could begin the healing process. In short, by flat out rejecting Stella's desire to goad Sarah into becoming her sparring partner in place of her husband, Sarah would avoid falling into her trap. If not, the sessions would be doomed from the start.

"Just answer my original question — what is it that makes your current husband strike you? I want to find out why this is happening to you. I am not here to save you from him because you are not as helpless as you think."

Stella's anger had not completely abated…her eyes still flashed daggers at Sarah, but she chose to placate her in a voice that sounded more like an impatient teacher, rather than a patient:

"Well, sometimes he comes home in a bad mood because something happened at work. I know he's going to take it out on me so I try to engage him in a conversation just to avoid being used as a punching bag. What's wrong with that?"

"Go on," Sarah persisted, trying to tamper down those angry emotions that were still aimed at her.

"So, after a while, he becomes more relaxed and starts to eat. He seems better so I bring up a point that has been bothering me — his lack of ambition and low pay. If the job is so awful, why doesn't he find another one, or if he is so indispensable that they are always coming to him to solve all of the problems, why doesn't he make more money? Is that such a terrible thing to say? I am only trying to help, but he doesn't want me interfering with his life! Every time I try to suggest that he do something — anything — about his job, he has a fit! The more I say, the more he screams until it ends with a whack!"

Sarah looked at her with arched eyebrows (she couldn't help it)…surely Stella could see that she was pushing his well-worn buttons, turning him into the "bad" one, allowing her to resume her saintly role in the relationship. Stella did not see it, at least not at first. Sarah knew she had to help her recognize the "good self-bad other" and "bad self-good other" dynamics that were caused by her early abuse, or she would continue to stumble down that same road. She had to learn to recognize the pattern, and eventually see how to change it in the future. Stella had to stop splitting herself and the other into all good or all bad. She had to learn to see that everyone has a good and bad side to themselves — which means that the image of the self has to be united and not split into all good and all bad parts at different times. Children see the world around them as either all good or all bad- the "good cowboys and the bad Indians," black and white rather than grey.

At the same time, Sarah had to actively avoid falling into the all-too-common sand trap of psychotherapy, which is to want so desperately to help the patient in any way possible that your desire to save the patient only confuses the situation. This would be especially difficult with Stella since her experiences so clearly shadowed Sarah's. She wanted to help her, but not in such a way as to be viewed by both of them as a savior. That would mean that if she rejected Sarah's help and sympathy (which she would most likely do since it would fly in the face of her own feelings of unworthiness and guilt), Sarah would begin to feel frustrated, and then angry at Stella for not accepting her assessment of the damage she was causing herself. This therapist-patient dynamic in turn would only lead both of them into further harm: Sarah would feel guilty about being angry at her and Stella would feel guiltless in much the same way she felt about her husband. As the "good" one, Stella would turn into the attacker and, as the "bad" one, Sarah would allow herself to be abused. Sarah could not allow herself to take on this role because if she did, Stella would soon fear retaliation from Sarah, thereby ending any possibility for her to heal.

Sarah was well aware that she would be treading dangerous ground throughout these sessions. Stella had aroused memories in her that were not only uncomfortable, but also risky for both of them. When Stella became depressed because she was aware that she was repeating the same mistakes in her second marriage that she had made in the first, she became angry with Sarah for what she saw as her placing all the blame squarely on Stella. Sarah was not really blaming her…that's just how Stella interpreted it. In actuality, Sarah was pointing out her contribution to the dynamic in order to help her heal both of them.

"Your difficulty at being able to accept your being angry with your husband instead of yourself is causing you to be depressed and guilty…but to make yourself feel better, you are trying to make me feel responsible for how you feel and then I will become the guilty one. I am not the one who is making you feel this way; I am showing you how to create a new pattern so that you can have a better relationship with your husband. The answer is not to walk away again, but to establish a self-awareness that will not only protect you from future abuse, but also stop it altogether."

I have to watch what I say to her…she may begin to see through my professional veneer and that would be a disaster for both of us. If Stella ever knew how closely her experiences mirror mine…my God, she even had the same manipulative mother who took joy in her daughter's defeats... she would look upon me as her equal. Instead of being her guide, I would become her cohort...someone with a sinful past as well--so who am I to judge her? Her eyes bother me...they hold me in a hypnotic stare, impelling me to confess my innermost thoughts and deeds so that she, the Priestess, could absolve me. I cannot allow her to control me, or turn me into her sex slave.

Yet, her vivid descriptions of physical abuse triggered something in me — an uncomfortable sensation that was nonetheless pleasurable. She had started me on a journey I thought I had finished long ago. I see now it was only momentarily suspended. It is absolutely crucial for me to get back on track before I am waylaid by Stella's mysterious powers. She speaks... and I react. If I turn the tables, then I could mold us both into a new image altogether.

Sarah steeled herself for what she knew would most likely be years of sessions with Stella. She was well aware that Stella would need this amount of time to heal, but she and Stella had to start somewhere. The key here would begin with their similarities, which Sarah could easily shape, and then reshape since her pattern nearly matched Stella's, much like those Simplicity Patterns in the 1950s...Stella would become a sort of prototype that was constantly in flux — never quite fixed, yet always evolving into a completely new model, but with classic lines. Sarah wove the threads, diligently reworking and refinishing the wavering outline because, when all was finally said and done, Stella was Sarah, and Sarah was Stella.

CHAPTER 3

BARRY AND GLADYS – THE MARRIED COUPLE
A PLAY IN 3 ACTS

<u>BACKGROUND/SETTING:</u>

Not long after the initial group meeting, Barry brought his wife Gladys for their first individual session with Sarah. While she had been conducting couple's therapy sessions for several decades, she still remained in awe of the increasing candor about such private matters as sexual relations, or lack thereof (remember, those were pre-Facebook and Twitter years). Sarah had been made uneasy of such revelations after her sessions with Stella. What stirrings would this fairly normal-looking man and wife incite in her? Sarah was hoping that what had happened to her during Stella's confessions was just a fluke, but she could not be too sure. With some trepidation, she watched Barry and Gladys enter.

Barry and Gladys are middle-aged, he being three years older than her. Married for twenty years (a shaky threshold for marriages — the "7 year itch" notwithstanding), they come from similar backgrounds (Jewish, but non-practicing) and had three children aged eight through fifteen. As a trained therapist, Sarah was used to expecting the unexpected; this couple was no exception. Meticulously dressed, (Sarah wondered if Gladys had selected Barry's perfectly coordinated cashmere sweater and silk tie with its russet and sage pattern that blended seamlessly with his trousers.) although slightly paunchy, Barry was still an attractive male with an interesting face. Gladys was equally appealing with blonde hair perfectly highlighted and skin that may have had a few Botox injections. She kept adjusting the line of her husband's pants...a hint of repressed desire, compulsive behavior, or both?

Gladys quickly reminded Sarah that Barry was a neurologist and she an elementary school teacher. They wished to present themselves as a professional couple from the start, as if to counteract what would follow. They quickly admitted that their sex life was non-existent, with sexual relations dwindling to an annual encounter on their anniversary. While the sex was perfunctory, each of them kept insisting that they still loved each other and wanted the marriage to continue. To this end, they both had tried individual therapy years earlier, which had helped them improve as individuals, but now they wanted to work together on fixing their marriage as a couple. They had begun working on this mutual goal with Diane, but had been dissatisfied with the results so they were eager to start again with Sarah.

Sarah soon discovered that Gladys is the emotional one-while Barry is the thinker... the over intellectualized one. Yet, Gladys retained a control verging on obsession over their household: the furnishings, social events, travel plans, and, most importantly, the children.

ACT ONE

GLADYS (in a whining, yet defiant tone):   He never shows any affection to me or the kids, but slobbers all over the dog!

BARRY (equally defiant): She always tells me what to do. She makes all the plans without ever consulting me.

GLADYS: Well, first he agrees to come, but then doesn't do what he says he will do — or he goes with me, but is never *with* me! (Collecting her thoughts for a moment) He's always withdrawn and cold.

BARRY: She tells me I should be more available to her and the kids and wants me to show my feelings. I keep my anger hidden most of the time, but eventually I explode in a rage. (In a voice louder than before) I have never hit her, but I often wanted to!

GLADYS (Her voice rising in a higher pitch and slightly louder than Barry's): Go ahead then! You'll never see me or the children again – I can promise you that. You shouldn't be the angry one here...I'm only trying to fix the relationship between you and me, and you and our children!!! (She appears on the verge of either crying or striking her husband.)

BARRY (Speaking in a glum voice): Well I end up feeling castrated by you and your attempts to fix me.

SARAH (in a voice deliberately spoken much lower than the others): First, let's talk quietly about your interactions and views of each other. That is the only way to even hear each other at all. I don't think you ever truly listen to each other. So, there will be no further outbursts in this room. Contain yourselves and try to put yourself in your spouse's shoes. Hear the other's feelings and thoughts from their position, not your own. Neither one of you is particularly empathetic to the other in the way companions usually are so let's try being nicer and calmer with one another, at least during the sessions.

You both need someone to witness what is happening between the two of you. My role here is as your mirror so that you can see for yourselves what is truly taking place. During our sessions, I will point out what I am aware of as you interact. That is why you are here. Both of you are so caught up in the dynamics between you that neither of you is able to step back to observe what is happening from a more objective point of view. I'll say it like I see it...my friends tell me I need better glasses! (All laugh nervously at the joke, which eases some of the tension in the room.)

SARAH (after the laughter subsides): Here's what I can tell at first glance - Gladys, you're trying to change Barry. It doesn't matter what we label it: fix, control, manipulate — it's all the same idea with the same effect. You are playing the all-too-familiar and self-destructive role of the "Controlling Female."

SARAH (looking at Barry): Barry, you're resisting what Gladys is trying to do in the only way you know how. You keep your anger submerged, but then it grows until you can't contain it. This conflict may have something to do with your overeating, which is something we can address at a later point. Part of your way of dealing with this possibly explosive situation is to resist passively — not aggressively or assertively. You say you will do something, but then don't, which is extremely frustrating to Gladys. You are playing the role of the equally self-destructive passive aggressive male... I'm sure you have both heard this term.

SARAH (Turning to Gladys): You, Gladys, grow more and more frustrated and then more and more angry and then try even harder to fix him. It never works and keeps repeating itself over and over. Old joke: HOW MANY THERAPISTS DOES IT TAKE TO CHANGE A LIGHT BULB? ONLY ONE—- BUT THE LIGHT BULB MUST WANT TO BE CHANGED. That principle applies here. Both of you need to work on your own part in what is now a dance of anger. Have any previous attempts worked?

BARRY AND GLADYS (at the same time): NO! (They look at each other, surprised at their rare concordance.)

SARAH (speaking firmly): So let's look at how you can change YOURSELF. I have another question here... Have either of you been able to stop or change the other? (Gladys and Barry shake their heads.) No? That's the very definition of "crazy": to keep doing the same thing with no success over and over again. You are not learning from experience, despite your above-average intelligence. Have either of you lived your life the way you wanted to? (Both ruefully shake their heads again.)

SARAH: Now, let's look at each of your contributions: Each of you is 100% responsible for your interactions. If either of you had not contributed 50% or not even 1% —the event would not have happened. (Speaking more firmly) *Own* your own thoughts and actions and DON'T BLAME anyone — not the other and not yourself. The only person you can change or control is YOURSELF. Look at your contribution and stop playing the BLAME GAME. Attributing blame to the other is just a way of getting yourself off the hook and to ignore your part in the problem at hand. What makes things worse is that each of you always wants to be RIGHT. That gets everyone nowhere. Instead, you must acknowledge the other's point of view and accept them for who they are. Acceptance is believed to be hugely important in many religions, as well as in the Kabbalah, and by atheists and psychologists alike. Can you see how these power and control issues are affecting your sex life as well?

Sarah is abruptly interrupted by a memory she thought had been swept out of her mind "SARAH – can't you do anything right for God's sake! I told you to bring my gray suit to the cleaners, but here it is hanging in the closet. You took my black suit, which was just dry-cleaned – I think you're losing your mind. Now the only dark suit left to wear is this heavy wool navy three piece and that's way too hot for June! I should have you committed – I'm going to do just that one of these days and no one will blame me. Everyone knows you belong there with all the other loons." That voice dipped in sneers was back inside my head, pelting me with lies. He had told me to take the BLACK SUIT!!! I knew it just as I knew my own name, but his skill at gaslighting was just surreal…a prime example of my second husband's coercive control over me.

SARAH (Her gaze returns, coming back into focus. She is back in the present.): You came here as a couple with your lagging sex drive as your most pressing problem, but that is just a symptom of the underlying relationship problems based on your specific personalities. Barry, you feel like she literally wants to castrate you and so you stay away from sexual intimacy as well. Gladys, you in turn feel that he doesn't want intimacy with you in any way.

Barry and Gladys pay close attention, noticeably interested in hearing what Sarah has to say.

SARAH (looking at her watch, momentarily uneasy by what she had recalled): At our next session, we will look at your personalities as the end product of a lifetime of experiences and early family interactions. This will allow me to show you how your past individual childhood experiences are still operating in the present because of your prior programming. Think of your brain as the computer with you as the sole programmer who can change the program. Each of our backgrounds influences us in the present moment even if we are not aware of how it does it…it is called the unconscious. So, you both need to become conscious of your pattern and contributions so that YOU are in charge of yourself. You don't need instructions or orders from anyone else, nor do you need to be the one who gives the orders. Thus you can choose the path in life you want. In essence, that is the reason you are here!!

(Gladys and Barry leave, each looking deep in thought. Sarah tries to shake off the disturbing memory, but instead her mind fast-forwards her to later scenes from her second marriage… being lashed emotionally into submission — not all that different from her first marriage filled with rage and physical abuse.

"Sarah, your mind is wandering again. I thought you had some intelligence — at least that's what you keep telling me. Maybe your parents knew you better than you think. You always seem to be off in La-La Land, never hearing what I am saying to you. I think you've taken on way too many responsibilities here — going back to school, seeing patients, leading group sessions. Why don't you just accept your own limitations? I'd be a happy man with you at home for a change, cleaning this dirty house and taking care of me the way a wife should." He drew me to him and gave me that look that he always used when he wanted to have sex. I usually gave in to him — he had a knack for making me feel guilty, yet turned on at the same time. What was that about anyway? I think I need to look back onto my own childhood along with Barry and Gladys. I thought I was done with all of this…

SARAH (alone): Why did I, a strong and free woman, allow myself to continue in those roles for so long? (She appears shaken, betrayed by her own remembrance of things past. She leaves her office, locking the door behind her.)

ACT TWO

After the first session and second group meeting with Barry, Sarah decides to prompt Gladys and Barry into their childhood remembrances to open up a few more windows into their present situation. She begins with Gladys, since she is the more forthright of the two.

SARAH (in a casual tone): What were your parents like?

GLADYS (with no hesitation): They were constantly arguing and so I took on the role of " Fixer," a habit I can't seem to break. I guess I was born to it.

SARAH (speaking gently): I will use the term Control Freak, but it is not an insult…I am using it more as a description. I used to be a control freak too because, like you Gladys, I wanted to make everything around me perfect. In fact, that is why I became a therapist — to solve the problems that I was unable to do as a child of combative parents. (Turning her attention to Barry) What about your parents?

BARRY (looking down at his shoes): My mother was cold and distant and my father was invisible. My mother pushed me to the limit, constantly berating and shaming me due to her own disappointments. Her face was frozen in a constant mask of regret — with me, my father, and herself. I was afraid to even breathe sometimes, knowing that the slightest thing would set her off.

SARAH: Such a home life left you with no model for assertiveness without anger. You had used your brain, as your mother had indoctrinated you to do, but you had to desert your emotions in order to survive. Those feelings are not gone completely; they are deeply buried within you, which may be why you overeat sometimes… feeding those emotions to keep them quiet.

GLADYS (breaking in stridently): I had a very needy mother and I felt it was my job in life to take care of her emotionally. So, when she was depressed, I was depressed as well…I wanted to reach her in any way that I could. I took charge to save her and now, I am taking on that same role in my relationship with Barry. A good example is when one of our children stays out past curfew. I stay up and worry while Barry just goes to sleep. Then I become angry with him because he shirks his responsibility, leaving me to deal with it all — the kids, the house, and my own career. It's just so stressful and totally unfair! But I suppose I am to blame…I want to save him just like I tried to spare my mother any grief. But I am still angry — with him and with myself.

(Sarah wants to help Gladys realize what is going on between Barry and her, but without bestowing blame.)

SARAH: So you, Gladys, are taking on all of the feelings and emotions in this relationship, and it's starting to take its toll on you. We have to deal with that situation, but first I want to inject another thought: "Opposites Attract" is a common theory and can be applied here because Gladys, as the emotional one, you are suppressing the thinking part of your brain. I do not mean that you are incapable of functioning in the world, but that your emotional brain leads your personality. On the other hand, Barry - you use your brain to think, but not feel…you are attracted to Gladys because of her ability to feel, not in spite of it. You identified more with your mother because you felt cut off by your impassive father. So Gladys stepped into the caregiver role, a familiar one for her since that is who she was to her needy mother. What makes things so difficult for Gladys is that she does not use the rational part of her brain to control her feelings. She continues to give and give of herself, hoping and expecting some kind of return. When that return does not happen, she becomes angry, just as she did with her mother. The role-reversal of Gladys as the parent and her mom as the child is very damaging in that there are both short and long term consequences.

GLADYS (assertively): Shouldn't Barry be more giving on an emotional level?

SARAH (more assertively): Try to eliminate the word "should" from your vocabulary. I know I am equally prone towards over-using it myself! That particular word leads to disaster here…you both find yourselves engaging in silly conflicts, like drinking directly from the milk carton or not closing the toothpaste, which leads to even more inane fights. It reminds me of a favorite *New Yorker* cartoon that featured a man and woman seated on opposite couches, with a duck sitting between them on the floor. The caption read, "THE DUCK STAYS!" It illustrates my point — people can argue about ANYTHING because they want to have control and power over the other person, BUT what you fail to realize is that the only one you can control is <u>yourself</u>…and that is extremely difficult, as you both know.

(While Sarah had hoped her attempt at humor would diffuse the tension in the room, Barry and Gladys go off on another tangent instead.)

GLADYS (ignoring Sarah, then badgering Barry): So where are we going for Rosh Hashanah - your family or mine? Your sister, Betty the Boob, is no Julia Child or even Colonel Sanders! If I have to eat her half-cooked chicken and risk salmonella again, I'll kill myself! And her kids! Such a bad influence — no manners whatsoever, never even looking at me when I talk to them! And if I try to correct them, Betty the Boob descends from her nest like a savage hawk, screeching and waving her arms at me. I can't take another holiday with that family…I don't care what you say!

BARRY (sarcastically): Oh, and that half-witted pack of idiots and imbeciles you call your family are so much more stimulating to be with! I have honestly never heard any one of them put more than three words together in a coherent sentence and those three words are rarely more than one syllable. The kids seem to be on drugs most of the time and the dog drools all over everything, but I guess that's par for the course when you live in a dung heap. (Turning to Sarah) I am not exaggerating here — the house is literally a pest hole!

GLADYS (face reddening and twitching with fury): Say one more word about my family and you'll see the back of me forever!

BARRY (in a quavering voice): Go ahead — make my day, as they say in the movies!

This ugly interaction stung Sarah…she and her two husbands also fought like cats and dogs, oftentimes ending with a hard smack on her face followed by a forceful coupling with her first husband, and a slammed door with her second husband.

"Sarah, you're just like your mother — that slatternly spoiled cow of a woman…what do you mean, you haven't made my dinner yet? Were you fooling around with that meter guy again? Open your legs wide – I want to smell your crotch for any left-over scum." I would willingly spread myself on the bed for him waiting for him to take me in his brutal way. I egged him on, fighting like a wildcat, because I knew it would make him come at me again and again. I was the one who pulled the switch, not him. That power was the ultimate aphrodisiac for me. It was the same with my second husband. He thought he was whipping me into submission emotionally, but I retained control and so I continued to engage both of them in this destructive way. I was aware of it then — just as I am aware of it now.

Sarah turns back to her patients, knowing she has to regain control of the situation before both storm out of the room.

SARAH: (jumping in quickly): Let's return to the concept of opposites attract…we all split off a part of ourselves while growing up in order to survive. The proper term for this is splitting. You fall in love with the person who embodies that submerged part, the missing piece, so to speak, because you need that part to make you a whole person. Then you try to change that person into yourself…sort of like that musical comedy "I Love You – You're Perfect – Now Change!" Splitting can make people believe: "I am the angel, you are the devil" or "I am the good one here — it's you who are the bad one." This is how children think — their world is black-and-white in terms of viewpoints…until they mature, which is what both of you need to do now. It is crucial that you develop an integrated self-image, not just of yourself, but also of your spouse. Neither one of you is the "bad one"…both of you are "good enough"…no one is perfect, nor should we expect them to be. With the exception of abuse or addiction issues, couples need to accept one another's flaws. In your relationship, these shortcomings are just minimal, when compared to other couples I have treated in this very room.

(Barry and Gladys looked at each other ashamedly.)

GLADYS: Sorry.

BARRY: Me too.

SARAH (speaking in a slow and deliberate manner): Since you both have expressed a desire to reconcile, which is half the battle, you must learn acceptance. The AA Serenity Prayer works here: "God, grant me the serenity to accept the things I cannot change…the courage to change the things I can…and the wisdom to know the difference." Even atheists understand the underlying wisdom; wisdom involves connecting thought with emotion on equal terms. You both need to take into account not just your own thoughts and emotions, but your spouse's as well. This is called 'mentalization,' the ability to understand what your spouse is thinking and feeling — true empathy.

BARRY (taking the lead for a change): Go on — you mentioned that term in our first group session, and I want to hear more about what it means.

SARAH: I will be happy to explain further. It is often the case that men take on the thinker role and women that of the feeler. Then, both sides try to get the other to change, but what we should be trying for is androgyny, that is to take on a part of the other. Anthropologists use ancient civilizations - where men hunted in the wilderness without speaking for days, while women gathered berries and spoke to one another - as scientific explanations for why the genders differ. This theory makes it seem as if the division is part of our inherited traits — a social DNA, so to speak. Yet, at this time, we should feel free to follow our own path, not some pre-ordained destiny. As it states in the Kabbalah, the Tree of Life always manifests itself as being balanced, moving towards the middle and away from the sides. You both need to work together on this balance, but I promise to address the sexual issue in our next sessions.

Barry and Gladys appear drained by this session. The outburst still weighing heavily on their minds, they walk out together, afraid to touch one another. Gladys leaves first and Barry quickly follows her.

For her part, Sarah knew she had laid the groundwork — now it was time to build upon it, not just for them, but also (as she now recognizes) for herself.

ACT 3

Barry and Gladys enter the room; their demeanor is uncertain, bordering on embarrassment. They know this session will focus on private matters, but the fact that they both are back shows that they not only trust the process, but also that they believe in themselves. Having gone through two grueling, yet enlightening sessions with

Sarah, they are now prepared to be open with one another and with her.

Since this session will confront their initial problem head-on, Sarah wants to avoid the trigger points that had disrupted the two previous sessions — no more petty arguments, no more blame games, and no more interruptions. She is counting on their willingness to try anything to save this marriage (including couples' therapy)! And so she feels optimistic about this next session.

SARAH (with determination): As much as I hate to return to what happened here last time, we do need to review what was said. Gladys, you taunted Barry about his family, especially his sister. You called her terrible names and insinuated that she had no respect for your opinions. Barry, you became enraged with Gladys. You poured oil upon the fire by calling her family idiots. That may have made you feel better for a moment, but I could see your regret afterwards. In fact, you both appeared abashed by your outbursts. You may not realize it, but that is the beginning of what I termed 'mentalization.' I hoped you worked on that since I last saw you because that ability will help bring balance into your relationship.

BARRY (in a dismissive tone): These psychological labels may work for your other patients, but I am really not that interested in all of that right now. I want you to delve into the nitty-gritty of what is happening to us sexually. (Raising his voice a notch) That is why I came to Diane's group in the first place. Since you seemed to be more in touch with this subject, I asked Gladys to give couples' therapy another try...and she agreed! I know that means something- something good in our marriage, but wanting to make things better and actually making them better are two separate matters. The reality here is that whatever I do in bed with her sexually is never right. She always complains that I don't touch her in the right places. She makes me feel so inadequate...like I need a sex manual at my age! It is so hard to want to touch her at all when all I hear is criticism and complaints coming out of her mouth.

GLADYS (quickly interrupting in a whining voice): Well, he doesn't try to please me, only himself! He has no concept of foreplay, just jumps right into it as if I am some kind of inflated doll! I almost feel as if he just wants to get it over with — like I'm not there at all.

(Sarah could feel their frustration with the situation…and with each other — so much pent-up sexual energy — it had to be diffused through the prism of analysis.)

SARAH: Can you see how the power and control dynamics that we have been speaking about are playing themselves out in your bedroom? Gladys, you want to retain an obsessive control over everything in your relationship, including your sexual experiences. By doing that, Barry steps into the passive aggressive role and refuses to give you what you truly want. Where is the balance there?

(Sarah sees that they had heard her on a physical level, but that they did not understand her on an emotional level. Convinced her words were too cerebral, she takes up Barry's challenge.)

SARAH: Tell me about your childhood sexual fantasies.

(After a brief uncomfortable silence, Gladys finally speaks.)

GLADYS (in a quiet voice that makes Sarah and Barry lean in to hear her): My fantasy was to be held captive in chains — a slave girl brought in to satisfy a warlord. I have to submit to his will…be totally captive.
   Gladys could be my long-lost sister — we both desire that total surrender…

SARAH: Barry, does what Gladys said come as a surprise to you?

BARRY (in a low drawn out whistle): Geez…I don't know what to say here.

SARAH (speaking only to Gladys): I am not at all surprised since I have heard similar scenarios from power-driven women. Girls your age were taught to stay virgins until marriage. That is why girls have to keep their desires and actions hidden, even from themselves. Gladys, you fantasize about having sex with someone who gives you no choice in the decision…you are being forced to participate- you did not initiate the encounter. The **Fifty Shades of Gray** trilogy, the film **Belle De Jour, The Story of O** – all of them deals with a similar story line. The fact that they attract a large audience should make you feel better. Rape fantasies are very common among women who would never want to be raped in real life.

Sarah tries to stop the images evoked by Gladys's description, but here they come:
She sees herself twirling in front of a full-length mirror, alone in her parents' apartment. She is a slave girl, dancing to please her master just as Scheherazade made up stories to amuse hers. Sarah sees herself in silken veils, smooth on her bare skin, deliciously anticipating the moment when her dance would lead to the bedroom where she would be ravaged.

(Sarah's eyes meet Gladys' in a brief moment of recognition.)

SARAH (reluctantly turning her gaze away from Gladys towards Barry): Please share your sexual fantasy with us. Be as openly honest as your wife was.

Barry had walked off to the side during Sarah's last speech to Gladys. He seems uncomfortable, yet intrigued by Gladys's revelation.

BARRY (haltingly): When I was a teenager, I fantasized about being with many women at once. They were all beautiful and racially different. A Chinese woman would be jerking me off, while a blonde with big breasts offered them eagerly to my mouth. A black woman and a plump redhead would be off to the side, watching us. Then they took over. I was the center of their physical attentions. Sometimes, they would have sex with each other and have me watch them go at it. Then I would join in the fun, screwing all of them at once! (Barry grins at the memory.) I still have these fantasies, except now I embellish the dreams by having them take turns stroking and licking my anus, sometimes even inserting a finger for a while. Afterwards one of them spanks me, while the other tells me I'm a naughty boy.   But I NEVER had sex with another guy! Never thought about it, even in my wildest fantasies!!!

SARAH (assuring him): Barry, what you have just revealed is perfectly normal among heterosexual men. So do not fear that erotic sensation in your dreams because you are not gay. The porn industry is intrinsically based upon this male desire…men having sex with two women, men watching two women having sex with each other and then having him join in, a dominatrix dressed in black leather whipping a disobedient sex slave – I'm sure I'm not shocking either of you. The fact is that no matter how deviant the scenarios, men feel right at home watching pornography, as long as a woman is present in the film.

(Barry looks invitingly at Gladys. She quickly glances back at him, in a sly way.)

SARAH (turning to the couple): Choose a porn film to watch together, not apart. Look for a film together — it should contain the elements of both your fantasies in it so that you can enjoy seeing it as a couple. Follow the same procedure with a book…take turns reading the parts aloud to each other. Next, talk to one another about your fantasies and then role-play. Gladys, you can be a slave girl with Barry as your master. Be the submissive one, not the one in control. You could even dress the part!

GLADYS (giggling girlishly): Barry, I can just see you in a warlord's outfit!

SARAH (speaking to Barry): This is what Gladys wants now — an assertive partner, not a man who remains passive and cool in the bedroom. On the other hand, men in positions of power, like you, desire switching roles just to relieve the stress of the outside world. So they want their partners to take over, just to give them a break from all of that responsibility. Some enjoy being with a dominatrix — the tabloids are full of political leaders involved in sex scandals that go beyond the norm - because that way, they are released from always being in the controlling position. However, Gladys is in control of your outside lives, which is why she needs you to be the master in the bedroom at times. (Shifting her attention to both of them now) This is where sexual role reversal comes into play - change your role by giving up the control and the power to your partner for a while — and then switch parts! Continue to take turns so that your life in the bedroom becomes more enjoyable. You will see then that your sexual satisfaction with each other will spill out into your lives outside the bedroom as well.

BARRY (nodding): OK, we'll give it a try this afternoon.

GLADYS (reaching for Barry's hand): Yes, we'll start right away. The kids won't be home for a few hours.

SARAH (firmly): Take it slow for now. Find a film or a book and just share it with each other as I described. Do not go too far too fast — that will only delay your progress.

(Gladys and Barry leave the session, their body language showing their eagerness to experiment with what they had found out about each other.)

SARAH (alone on stage) There is still much to work on with them, but their new sexuality is stimulating — so contagious…She closes her eyes.

Here I am again-surrounded by a swirl of color…back in time to my girlhood fantasies. I feel warm and comfortable inside, but then a familiar sense of unease intrudes my daydream. Have I somehow been discovered in my reverie, as I had by my parents all those years ago? There I was, twelve years old, on the brink of sexuality, playing an innocent game of Spin-the-Bottle, anxiously anticipating my first real kiss from a male who was not a relative. He was a gorgeous guy with black hair, strong mouth, and a bulging crotch. I couldn't wait for him to engulf me! But then I felt a cold wind at my back and disturbingly familiar voices pecking at me like angry crows…my parents swooped into the room, dragging me away in front of everyone — all the while spitting out epithets like "slut" and "whore." The memory still brings a blush of shame to my cheeks.

SARAH (opening her eyes and facing the audience): Their strict control over me included no make-up, no dating, and no freedom at all! Their strict rules culminated in my being out of control as a teenager. Oral sex with a number of boys, just because I believed it would make me popular, led to date rape at the age of fifteen.

Sarah closes her eyes again, head bent:
Ron paws at me, his stronger body getting the better of me with ease. I lay crumpled on the front seat of his father's car, parked on a hidden road inside of Alley Pond Park, as he roughly pulls himself out of me. My legs are all sticky…my insides ache…and my heart is broken.

SARAH (opening her eyes again, looking straight ahead): Where was the romance of the First Time I had read about in books? Yet, I continued on in that horrific relationship, justifying my actions as those of someone in the throes of true love, if only to protect myself from believing my parents' opinions of me. This pattern of unfulfilled relationships would continue until I was able to stop the cycle once and for all, but not until I had survived two abusive marriages and, after thirty years of ongoing therapy, learned how to use my hard-won victories to help others.

These sessions with Barry and Gladys continued through several years, in couples' therapy and with Barry in the group sessions, as they returned for refresher treatments when their family dynamics changed. As they worked through their conflicts, Sarah reaffirmed her own hard-won victories; their desire to improve not only strengthened her resolve, but also validated her as an effective and guiding therapist.

CHAPTER 4

PAULINE THE LADY-IN-WAITING

When Pauline had mentioned that she was looking to have a child through a surrogate mother, Sarah's ears perked up…she had gone through a similar experience (not a walk in the park, especially since Sarah chose to go that route over thirty years ago), and so she was looking forward to their individual sessions together, away from the group. Putting it simply, Sarah wanted to forge a bond with this woman, who could easily have been her at a younger age. She wanted to give her the benefit of her expertise in this particular field…the thought appealed to her wish to help others and to dispel some of her recent disquietude. She did not realize then that this relationship would be a symbiotic one.

Pauline does not appear at all nervous in her initial individual session, unlike some of the other patients in the group. In fact, her question was direct and open:

"I'm not sure whether to use a surrogate or just adopt a child. My husband and I do not have any kids and I'm infertile."

Sarah eagerly responds by commiserating with her:

"I understand it's a difficult decision and very complicated. What is your thinking on the subject?"

Being a pragmatist, Pauline addresses the practical issues first, "Well I don't think it's legal in New York to use a surrogate. It may be easier to just adopt a child here."

She had a good mind, analytical and focused on reality, not the emotions behind it all. Yet, Sarah's instincts told her that Pauline was more emotional than she let on. Nevertheless, Sarah chose to follow her lead by beginning with pertinent facts from her own life:

"I went through the same thinking process years ago. Do you remember the Baby M case? Mary Beth Whitehead was the surrogate mother; her story became newsworthy because she refused to give the baby up to the parents who had contracted with her through a lawyer to use the husband's sperm and the surrogate's egg. It was headline news, not only because of the pros and cons of the case, but also because surrogacy was a fairly new concept at the time."

Pauline draws a blank so Sarah fills in more details:

"The lawyer had had Mary Beth first tested by a psychologist, but he did not divulge the findings to the parents. The testing had shown that Mary Beth was a borderline personality and thus might present some difficulties down the road. Once the baby was born, she did not have the emotional health needed to give up her child, and so the case was brought to court. The judge awarded the parents "Baby M," but gave Mary Beth visitation rights, which completely confused the child. For example, Mary Beth used a different name for the child when she was with her. So it became a very muddled situation for all concerned. Unlike the selfless real mother who surrendered her maternal rights rather than have her baby cut in half in the book of Solomon, Mary Beth could not and would not understand how such a decision could hurt her child."

My memories of Baby M raised that old familiar anxiety within me again.

Sarah immediately reverts back to her original train of thought, fearful of Pauline's powers of perception.

"Do you know what a borderline personality is?"

Pauline asks Sarah to please explain the term, although Sarah is certain she is familiar with the word itself since it was bandied about so much in the media.

"There is a continuum of normality or abnormality in personalities. On one end sits psychosis, which means being out of touch with reality as most of the world sees it, and on the other end there is normalcy, even though no one truly knows what normal is. Toward the psychotic end of this continuum lies a 'borderline personality,' which is a person who displays some very seriously disturbed personality traits, such as being highly manipulative."

Stella in all of her glory! Why didn't I recognize a dyed-in-the-wool borderline personality speaking directly to me the other day? She is so much more of a disturbance to my state of mind than I first realized — another layer to peel away...

Sarah makes a mental note to return to this new insight on Stella, after Pauline leaves. She continues her explanation on the borderline personality, perhaps more for her own sake rather than for Pauline's:

"For example, if a loved one expresses a desire to separate from such a personality, then he/she will threaten suicide to prevent that person from leaving. Borderline personalities often have mood disorders and irrational thoughts, but they are not quite as over the edge as schizophrenics."

Perhaps not wanting to delve so much into psychological issues right now, Pauline presses Sarah for more facts on Baby M:

"So why didn't the lawyer tell the parents?"

Sarah is able to provide Pauline with minute details since it was a case with which she had far too much expertise. She finds herself reliving the decades-old events as if they had just happened the month before.

There my husband and I sat in that office that appeared just a little too slick, pouring our hearts out to a well-shaven man with a long crow-like face. He smiled, never showing his teeth, yet could still manage to grin from ear to ear. His voice was conspiratorial, which made the entire transaction smack of illegality. All we wanted was a baby to share our lives, but he managed to take all of the hope away, while still offering us all of the answers. His mannerisms still make my skin crawl...

Sarah shakes off the unpleasant image and continues her account:

"The lawyer was more interested in making the deal so he could earn his fee. His malfeasance made things very hard for me because at the same time, my husband and I were deciding whether or not to use a surrogate much like you, and actually went to the same lawyer who had mishandled the Baby M case. Of course, we were not aware of all the brouhaha at the time. He appeared quite connected and had a large file with scores of women wanting to be surrogates. He was willing to provide us with all kinds of information, except of course their names. He insisted that we sign a contract with him and then he would separately sign a contract with the surrogate. This lack of contact with the surrogate made us uncomfortable so we contacted an attorney friend, who strongly suggested that we find the surrogate on our own, which we did. We advertised anonymously in several newspapers and eventually found someone whom we had tested first to ensure her emotional stability. Next, we hired our own lawyer who drew up a contract between us and the surrogate. As it turned out, we were the first and the last couple in New York State to have a child through a surrogate. Due to the Baby M case, the courts had decided surrogacy was illegal. Now there are only some states in the US where it is legal. So if you decide to go down that road, you would have to go to a different state, which of course makes it even more difficult. Speaking about it here as I just did makes it sound very cut and dry, but there were strong emotions that fluctuated among all of us involved, including the surrogate mother."

I am still astounded by what we accomplished-all of the legalities, the back-and-forth discussions, the overall strain on us, and finally the birth of that beautiful baby…a true miracle.

While Pauline is closely following the narrative, she appears torn so Sarah asks, "What is your thinking about using a surrogate versus adopting?"

Pauline reveals her own primal fears,

"Well, it may be better for the child to have some genes that came from at least one of its parents. I am sterile, but my husband's sperm is fine."

After a deliberate pause, Pauline leans her body towards Sarah while trying to judge whether or not to reveal a deeper truth about her past. She gives Sarah a searching look and then continues:

"Now, I have something to tell you that is highly confidential. I have had an abortion…that is the first time I said that aloud to anyone. The memory of it is just so overwhelming. It was a long time ago – I was a scared teenager, terrified that my father would never forgive me. So, without telling anyone a thing about it — not even my boyfriend – I went to a clinic and just had the baby whooshed out of my body. At the time, I felt no guilt, just joyous relief – How could I have been so unthinking or unfeeling!"

Burying her head in her hands, Pauline's grief spills out of her eyes. Sarah reaches out to her, wanting desperately to comfort this shattered woman before her, but, not wanting to be interrupted, Pauline inhales back her tears and goes further:

"Now this whole awful situation has unburied the child I murdered. Perhaps I cannot bear another one as a punishment — no, not perhaps — definitely! At a young age, I learned that God poured sorrows down upon those who had sinned — oh, yes, he was a vengeful master, much like my strict father who devised unholy methods of corporal castigations for me. He made me bend over in front of a picture of the Virgin Mary, whipping me with a belt as I was forced to recite the Hail Mary three times. If I rushed through the prayer in order to lessen the amount of strikes, he would grab me by the hair, push up against me and bite my breasts until they bled. His eyes were full of lust – I recognized it even as a young girl. But he never raped me. He was a sexually frustrated deviant who never acted on his impulses. I know that now, but I still can't rid myself of this guilt."

Sarah knows she has to make Pauline feel less guilty about what she had done. She was about to commiserate with her through a past shared experience, but something inside stopped Sarah from what she was going to say. Pauline's experiences, while even more horrific than her own, did hold a whiff of recognition for Sarah. She was far too frightened to revisit her father's study in her mind, at least not so soon after her sessions with Stella. Her instincts told her to hold back from Pauline at this point because she felt her strength ebbing away…she knew she had to keep herself safe if she was going to be useful to Pauline…and so Sarah held her tongue. Instead, she repeated well-accepted truths she had both learned and passed on in past therapy sessions:

"Pauline, your first priority has to be you. If you had borne that child, what would have been the results? You would not have completed your education, you would have been shunned by your God-fearing family, and you probably would not have been able to support the child. Your resentment would have turned you into an uncaring, if not dangerous mother…we have seen such cases in the news…or you would have ended up in a bad marriage, with a husband who would have humiliated both you and your child because he had heroically come to your rescue! Most likely, he would be a clone of your father, eventually making you wish that neither you nor your child had ever been born. But instead, here you are, a well-educated and fairly well-adjusted woman in a happy marriage with a kind and loving husband that you so well deserve. Don't you think you are better off this way?"

Pauline seems as if she wants to believe Sarah, but she still clings to the idea of her unworthiness:

"The truth of the matter is that I am an infertile woman. I know in my head that I am not less of a woman, but in my heart of hearts, I feel diminished, not keeping up my end of the marriage relationship. My husband should have married someone without such a checkered past, but of course he doesn't know what I did. But, instead of being grateful for a positive way out of the problem that I caused, I can't help feeling bitter. After all, while it may be a better solution for my husband and the child, I still feel hurt by the whole arrangement. Will this child really be a part of me?"

Her question and repetition of the word "may" are enlightening — she had misgivings (*and oh, how that mixed bag of emotions was so achingly familiar...*), so Sarah knows she needs to answer Pauline honestly and clearly. Hearing her own ideas repeated back to her from so many years ago, Sarah empathizes with her patient in a way she never had with other patients:

"I completely understand that line of thought." Sarah then offers Pauline a supportive sense of optimism. "In our case, it worked out beautifully because our son resembled my husband and his family so it was easier for him to fit in with us — even though he didn't look at all like me. Before we told him about the surrogacy, he had asked me a number of times why he didn't have anything physically in common with me or any of my family. My husband and I were always in conflict about when and what to tell him, but anyone who adopts a child has to face the same questions and decisions."

Pauline's interest is palpable. "So when did you tell him and how did he react?"

I vividly remembered the conversation and how afraid I was of what he would say, this ten-year-old boy whose curiosity was embedded in his DNA.

"He accepted it completely. He just asked a few questions like: "Was she pretty and smart? and 'Will I ever meet her?' We told him that when he turned eighteen, he would have the choice of whether he wanted to meet her. Then he nonchalantly replied to what we had believed would be a traumatic experience for him, 'Mom - take me out in the kayak."

I suddenly relished once more that soothing balm he had given me, coupled with a liberating release from the fears that had gripped me deeply inside for so long. That kayak ride matched my absolute joy in the world at that moment!

"When he reached eighteen, he decided he didn't want to meet her after all, and never did. He saw me as his mother, which I was and still am. The person who cares for the child daily is the one who makes the connection; she is the mom. So whether you adopt or use a surrogate will not really make much of a difference. I know that now because I went through the initial fears and trepidations, just like you are now, but I came through whole on the other side."

And so I did, didn't I!

Sarah touches Pauline's arm, but still sees the anxiety on her face. Sarah knew it all too well.

Pauline speaks quietly, again resisting the urge to weep,

"But I'm afraid that the child would feel closer to my husband than to me because they will have that genetic connection."

Speaking again from experience, Sarah assures her:

"Maybe but that's not the only relevant point. What will be important is how close you become to the child, and how much love and caring you show towards him/her. My son always felt loved by both of us. That is why he tells anyone easily about his background... and especially that he feels like he was a completely desired child — not just an accident, or given away because he was not wanted. Over the years, we revealed more details so that he would know how hard it had been for us to go through the process. Hence, he felt truly wanted by both mom and dad!"

Pauline again brings up a practical point:

"I'm also afraid that the surrogate might have a tough time giving up her child. I was afraid that first time that I would not be able to give up my baby for adoption so I made the decision to abort it instead. At least that's what I told myself."

Sarah chose to address Pauline's more detached concerns about the amorphous surrogate with answers based on scientific research. She knew that approach would appeal to Pauline:

"You are correct to recognize that it seems to go against all we know of motherhood to give away a child, but one of my students did a research dissertation on the attachment level of pregnant surrogate mothers compared to pregnant mothers who plan on keeping their child. The published findings showed that the attachment of the surrogate mother to the unborn fetus was much less than that of a mother who is keeping the child. So although such an act can be hard, it is still easier than just giving your child away for other reasons, such as not being able to take care of it… because that would add feelings of parental guilt and inadequacy to the equation. As to your choice of an abortion over adoption, an adopted child might feel a greater sense of abandonment than that of a surrogate child, since most surrogates do not only give their child away for money, but also for a more altruistic reason; that is providing a service to mothers who are unable to have a child of their own."

Pauline is skeptical, asking pointedly, "Wouldn't the surrogate child still feel abandoned by his/her biological mother?"

Once more, Sarah must hasten to address her concerns with facts gleaned from scientific research:

"Feelings of abandonment are far less likely when the child is born through surrogacy. Why? Because he knows why he was created and where he came from. Another of my graduate students, who was an adopted child, wrote her dissertation on the abandonment issue. Many adoptees find themselves questioning why their mother gave them away. Was there something wrong with them?

Worst of all-were they unloved? This particular doctoral student was unsure of her origins so she interviewed other adoptees, only to find that many of them were experiencing the same difficulties. They often longed to meet their biological parents, or at least be told information about them and why they gave them away."

Sarah knows she is making some headway with Pauline so she perseveres:

"Moreover, when there are two unknown biological parents rather than just one, more is left to question. A great deal of research has been done on the effects adoption has on adoptees. So much more is unknown about birth mothers in a regular adoption situation than in a surrogate birth. In the latter case, the parents are able to provide their child with crucial information to satisfy their inquiries and concerns. The older child may even have the chance to know or meet her.   So you see, in many ways surrogacy makes the journey easier for the child than the adoptive way. The decision to meet her lies in his/her hands, which means a greater sense of control. It is called empowerment, which makes a person feel more at ease — don't you agree?"

Pauline nods vigorously in agreement,

"I'm becoming more convinced so I will discuss the possibility further with my husband. But to be completely honest, right now I'm still shaky and unsure about my ultimate decision. I appreciate your sharing so much of your own life with me. Your openness and empathy are new to me. Diane had a different style; she did not reveal as much information about herself. I guess she was keeping a professional distance."

Sarah felt she had redeemed herself; she had made an important breakthrough with Pauline, and so Sarah feels comfortable in her acknowledgement of the connection between them:

"I know what you are saying. When I first began supervising other therapists, I always recommended that they not talk about themselves during sessions because that is when it is the patient's time to talk and share. Yet, over the years, I concluded that there are times when it is appropriate for a therapist to share certain experiences as long as the therapist is not asking the patient for advice. Believe it or not, I have seen some therapists do just that, leading to an unhealthy role reversal. I think that you realize that I was not asking for your help just now. I decided to reveal information about myself to you because I believed it was pertinent to your situation and therefore, might be helpful to you. It is important for you to recognize that everyone, including your therapist, is likely to have problems just like you and everyone else in or out of therapy. Are you comfortable knowing what you now know about me?"

Sarah is relieved by Pauline's response:

"Yes, I feel very comfortable with you because you do not put yourself above me… on a pedestal so to speak… even though you do have it all put together."

Little did Pauline know that our session was mutually therapeutic. She had reminded me of how strong I had to be way back then…confronting what I thought were my inadequacies and then rising to conquer those challenges of self-worth, self-pity, and self-doubt. As they used to say, "You've come a long way, baby!" I had taken on the emerging field of surrogacy with all its moral and legal questions and had made it my own. In that way, I now understood that I was my son's true mother. I had fought the good fight for him, just like any mother and I deserved the rewards.

Sarah turns away from her feelings of elation and focuses again on Pauline:

"During my sessions, I tend to use everything from my own life and experiences — not just what I learned from my training. We are all humans, in conflict with ourselves, our mates, our children, our extended families, our friends, and the outside world. It is important that we embrace that commonality; it allows us to survive. I have one last piece of information for you regarding surrogacy: I just read a recent interview with Baby M; she's doing very well — despite her birth mother's intrusions. This just confirms my belief that children born from surrogates can do just fine. See you next week."

As Pauline departs the session, Sarah regrets not having revealed more of herself to this particular patient — she and Pauline shared so many things.

As I was stretched out upon the cold metal table in an uncomfortable and awkward position, I looked up at the ceiling. Silly platitudes had been pasted all over its surface, by whom I had no idea. Were they put there as a distraction or were they intended to impart hidden messages to us, the unwilling, anxious and terrified girls and women? One in particular struck me as being particularly pointed: A Stitch in Time Saves Nine. Hah! I suppose that was meant to be a pithy joke — have an abortion now to save you nine months of shame. I was participating in an immoral act, according to much of society and, in particular, my parents. All I wanted was to have this whole mess cleaned up so I could go out and enjoy myself here in the Poconos. My boyfriend was impatiently waiting outside — he had forced me into sex at exactly the wrong time so he had to pay the price. I was well worth the 500 bucks — he was going to make sure of that! As I entered the ether cloud, I saw my parents' faces contorted into those of snarling tigers...I made a promise then that I would never tell another soul about this.

After the procedure, we went exploring in the caves, fooling around with one another as best we could. I never gave my baby a second thought...but now, I am haunted by his beautiful face every day.

My second abortion had to take place, no ifs, ands or buts about it. This pregnancy occurred after a barbaric rape by my first husband. He had punched me senseless after an ugly argument and then had proceeded to sodomize me while I was unconscious. The force of being anally raped brought me back to my senses FAST! I had to get him out of me...I felt like I was being ripped apart so I found the strength to turn over and let him enter my vagina instead. I remember thinking about the timing and the likelihood of pregnancy, but I was in survivor mode. So, when I found out I was indeed pregnant, I got rid of it quickly without telling anyone, just like Pauline. This time, I was deeply ashamed and guilty…it wasn't the poor baby's fault that I remained in this abusive relationship. I sought comfort in believing that his father would probably choke him and kill him anyway… so I was saving him from a cruel fate, wasn't I? No, not really… I had deliberately committed matricide twice and the horror of it is truly unbearable. Pauline spoke of her sterility being a punishment…she was right, of course, at least about me. She was at least remorseful, but I only felt badly much later on. I suppose I was watching out for myself rather than the unborn child — something I tell all of my patients in that situation. It's good therapy, but then why do I feel so distraught again?

CHAPTER 5

CATHERINE THE MEDDLER

Catherine walks quickly into her therapy session — her body stance and facial expressions matching her abrupt manner, and even more on display here than at the first group session. She had bitterness deepening the harsh lines on her face and a mouth drawn into a downwards grimace, much like that of a dejected marionette. What was it that made her so dismal? Sarah had read Diane's notes, but somehow they did not delve deeply enough to satisfy her. Today, at this moment, something had set Catherine reeling and she could hardly wait to spit it out:

"My daughter-in-law is always angry with me. She is always demanding something from me-money, babysitting duties, chauffeuring her, the children or all of them somewhere, and so many other tasks that they make my head whirl! You see, she is quite the hypochondriac — always going to one doctor or another to find a cure for what I like to call the 'Disease of the Month.' If she hears anything on the news about some epidemic or mysterious ailment…Zika, Ebola, West Nile, Lupus…you name it — she's got it! The slightest headache and she's convinced she is at the end stages of brain cancer, or perhaps it is an aneurysm lurking inside of her, just waiting to burst. My son caters to her every whim or fear, even the most outlandish ones! I just cannot understand their marriage. At first, I gave in to her wishes just to keep peace with her and my son. Now I believe that course of action was a big mistake because now whenever I refuse to help out since I have a life too, she becomes furious with me-calling me a selfish bitch who has no love of family! She never appreciates anything I have done for her-never even a word of thanks, much less any physical show of gratitude like a simple hug — so I am constantly at odds with her."

As Sarah waited patiently for Catherine to finish her harangue, Catherine kept looking at Sarah in desperation. She ended by blurting out, "I need your help on how to handle this situation."

Sarah thought about it and then decided to first address what could be going on with the daughter-in-law, without placing blame on Catherine:

"She may have somewhat of a personality disorder. On the normality continuum, she sounds as if she may be nearer the psychotic end, but not quite. People like that are known as 'borderlines' — they have difficulty understanding or empathizing with others. Borderlines can only view everything from only their own perspective and generally overreact to the small stuff. That is why your daughter-in-law truly believes she is deadly ill; her thoughts are real to her, no matter how incredible they may appear to you and other people in her life. They are also unable to think things through clearly, and so they are quick to pull the trigger — mainly because they lack the ability to fully comprehend the other's motives."

Maria, my college roommate, lies in bed yet again with one of her "unbearable" migraines. I remember how the curtains were always tightly drawn to kill the sunshine by day and the lights of the city by night. Our apartment's funereal aspect was unsettling to everyone who ventured into it, including my lovers, but that was the least of my worries. Going to any restaurant with Maria, even a kosher deli, gave her stomach cramps that were "positive signs of food poisoning." That meant another all-night stay in the local ER…usually hours before an important exam. How I grew to resent and loathe Maria! She would claim to have periods of out-of-body paranormal activity in which she would "float above herself," and then have a difficult time re-entering her own body! I realize now that she was a deeply disturbed young woman, but at the time, I just wanted out of this weird freakish existence so I moved several blocks away from her. For years and even now, I feel guilty and ashamed that I had abandoned her to her fate: years in an asylum that ended with her jumping to her death into the chilly waters of the Hudson. Her face is frozen in a silent scream as she hits the dark water…why didn't anyone tell her it would hurt so much? Why wasn't anyone there to rescue her? Now as a trained therapist, I feel I should have been there for her. Well, let me at least attempt to help another young woman like Maria by at least guiding Catherine through this dilemma.

With that thought echoing in her head, Sarah proceeds to explain further:

"For example, one of my borderline patients became unhinged when her friend failed to call her on her birthday. It did not occur to her to find out what may have happened to cause this unexpected affront… her friend may have been going through some difficulties, like an illness or emergency of some sort, but my patient was so apathetic that she would not even try to find out what happened. She truly believed that she knew what her friend was about, but in fact her personality blocked out any understanding of her friend. That is so much like your daughter-in-law; she doesn't see you as a caring and giving person. Catherine, do you think you are a caregiver?"

The question made Catherine's face soften for the first time since Sarah had met her:

"Yes, - I think I am. Everyone else has always said that about me… that I often take care of others, but not myself."

She thought about it a little more:

"But, you know, I don't see myself that way! Whenever another person accuses me of not caring, I find myself believing them."

Sarah rebuts with one of her first rules for her patients:

"What I am about to tell you is so important for you to understand. On planes, we are all instructed to place the oxygen mask on ourselves before placing it on a child. That rule is put there so that passengers will remain conscious and thus be able to save their child if the need arises. You must first help yourself in order to save someone else. I like to use this example with everyone who is an *over-giver.* Remember that it is you who must take care of yourself first and then the other. In the Kabbalah exists the Tree of Life, with one of its branches called "Givingness," which of course is crucial in any religion and life, but there is one side that is the force… and the other side that is the structure that prevents the force from overextending itself. Your giving-ness has to settle into the middle of the tree — or you will not have anything left to give."

Catherine objects to the analogy, as Sarah suspected she would, "But that makes me feel selfish. Isn't the idea of 'watching out for number one' the epitome of selfishness?"

"No - it's taking care of you for the good of others. That is not being selfish. Tell me how you feel when you say "no" to anyone."

Catherine confesses, "I feel guilty — something inside me dictates that I should always do whatever the other person wants."

Sarah hesitates before asking the next question. It was a natural follow-up to Catherine's last statement, but an old feeling of uneasiness simmered just below the surface of her consciousness:

"How did your mother treat you?"

Catherine's answer doesn't surprise Sarah:

"She was not very giving. To be honest, I had to take care of her or she would rage at me, calling me selfish and ungrateful. Her favorite expression was that old one…you know…how one mother can take care of ten children, but ten children can't take care of one mother. I became so sick of hearing her say that, as if she was the image of motherhood, but she wasn't — not at all! Most of the time she just sat in her favorite chair, watching mindless soap operas and shushing me if I dared speak to her. I think I hated her."

Catherine's intensity frightens her. Had she just said that she hated her mother? Sarah could see the physical and psychological ramifications taking place… GUILT forcefully held both therapist and patient in its claw-like grasp.

Sarah! You are such an evil child…Why don't you ever listen to me? I can't take it anymore! I'm going to tell your father to throw you in a locked room while he is at work. You'll see who the boss around here is — it's not you, it's ME and it will always be me! My mother's voice and words shrilled in my ears. I remembered my own intense hatred of that woman who claimed to be my mother. I saw her slumped on the floor in that familiar fetal position-so dramatic! My father came home, the doctor was called, an injection was administered to her, while I was forced to be a witness to the tragic events I had caused. Then having to crawl on my hands and knees to beg her forgiveness — preceded by the initial subjugation of my father's firm yet erotic spanking- with me never truly feeling any regret…only a fervent wish that she would disappear from my life."

Sarah pulls back from that scathing memory. She looks at Catherine with new eyes. She struggled to hold onto that façade she had carefully constructed of herself as an unflappable therapist. She carefully reacts to Catherine's last outburst:

"I know you are horrified by what you just said, but let's explore why you are feeling that way. We internalize feelings based upon our childhood…in other words, we take in the image of the person who was our mother or caretaker. We have this image of ourselves in relation to her in the dyad: self and other, with one as the giver and the other as the taker. Since you had to take on the role of giver even at an early age because your mother would not show love to you if you did not, you later became the caregiver to others in your life, but without a balanced view. She did not take care of you the way you take care of others now. This is also called a reaction formation. Your mother acted one way and you reacted in the other way. Children see the world in terms of black and white- like cowboys...the "good " ones wore white and the "bad" ones wore black, but there must actually be a gray way of perceiving the world. You should not be all good or all bad; that is how children think. However, I am not saying that you are a child –what I mean is that within you exists the internalized self and other people's images of you that you have taken in as a child. One is the bad one and the other is the good one. You are always trying to be the good one and if you are accused of being the bad one, your reaction is to internalize it. Do you often find that you defend yourself during arguments?"

This lengthy monologue gives Catherine the time she needed to unwind a little,

"Yes, I am always defending myself or trying to justify my behavior to myself as well, but most of the time I end up believing the other's negative perception of me."

Sarah then labels her feeling to provide Catherine with a sense of normality:

"That is known as 'introjective identification', a fancy term that means that when one person in a dyad projects his or her own feelings, the other one takes them in. Have you noticed that kind of behavior at other times in your life?"

Catherine nods vigorously,

"Yes, I remember studying hard for a test, but my friend hadn't. Yet, knowing that made me the anxious one. I became so nervous going into the test even though I was the one who had studied like crazy, but she seemed calmer."

Sarah practically shouts,

"That's it in a nutshell! Projective identification and introjective identification. It takes two to tango"

Not to be distracted in her quest for a solution, Catherine then returns to the troubling subject of her daughter-in-law:

"She often tells lies for no reason at all... why?"

Now Sarah is in a comfortable position again — that of a trained therapist...*here is my chance for me to make amends for my neglect of Maria...*

"People-most especially borderlines-often lie without even being aware that they are lying. They fantasize and are unable to distinguish between the fantasy and what really happened.   They make up a tale and end up believing it themselves. They are not liars per se — just people who believe the lies they tell themselves. Remember those oxygen masks... the most important thing you can do to save others is to work on you first."

Catherine is not all that convinced:

"Yes, but I'm worried about my grandchildren. I think that is why I interfere so much. How will her behavior affect them?"

Sarah persists,

"I understand your fears, but you can never change another person. Look how hard it is for you to change even though you are in therapy; the fact that you are here and in the group proves that you want to heal, but if someone does not seek help in changing their patterns, you can never fix them. In fact, borderline personalities have adapted their behaviors to help them cope with their inner problems. Whatever factors formed the borderline personality-background, experiences, genes, etc., — they are who they are and they absolutely refuse to accept any changes suggested by others, which is difficult for people like you and me to accept because we are fixers. My friend calls me a meddler-I have to see that movie called The Meddler! My children have called me a manipulator, an interferer, a micro-manager, but I call myself the fixer."

Sarah, who are you kidding? Catherine and I share an obsessive compulsion disorder — she wants to control her family by making them over in her own perfect image, even if that means destroying her son's marriage in the process. She is unwilling to surrender her control over him. For me, I refused to give in to orgasms for a very long time because they made me feel that I was not in charge of my own body. Eventually I had to find help from a sex therapist who showed me how to fully enjoy an orgasm without fear…

Sarah knows she must give Catherine more explicit directions in order to succeed in her own quest for redemption:

"It took me a long time to see that you cannot change others — only yourself. If you keep trying to remake her into what you think she should be, then you will not get anywhere because that is the road to failure each and every time. In what way do you think you might be able to improve your behavior towards your daughter-in-law?"

Catherine reacts defensively at first, but then thinks it over and concedes,

"Why should I change what I'm doing when she is the one who should be in therapy? But, now that we've talked awhile, I must admit that… I never thought about it that way. I'm always trying to get *her* to be different. That was probably the wrong approach because I see now that my raging with her has affected my son."

Reassured by Catherine's response, Sarah prods her to go further — "How?"

"He's constantly pleading with me to stop arguing with his wife. It gets him into trouble with her because he's in the middle and he feels that he has to take one of our sides. Of course that is never an easy position to be in and it always hurts him in the end."

Once again, Sarah regains her position of authority,

"Here I agree 100%. That's what happens in a triangle — the one in the middle is always in conflict, not knowing who to side with, and of course the other two sides eventually get mad at the middle one for taking the other's side-even when he is struggling to be fair to both. What it all boils down to is your acceptance of the fact that your daughter-in-law is who she is, for better or worse. Stepping into her arena will only cause trouble for you and for your son. Whenever she tries to involve you, you have to step back and not engage her because you will never win that battle. You spoke earlier about your concerns for your grandchildren. I understand, but the only thing you can do is to show them love and caring, and to be there for them when they ask for help. Resist criticizing their mother since your disapproval will set them against either you or her; the more stress in the family, the worse it will be for all of you, including your daughter-in-law. When there is additional conflict, the borderline is in danger of falling down into the abyss. We will talk further on how to better understand her and how you can change your behavior to help her and your family."

Sarah grows even more confident after her temporary setback. If I only knew then what I know now — an old adage, but it is especially applicable now. My training could have helped Maria; she would have been alive today!

Catherine is now showing more concern about her daughter-in-law instead of her initial rage: "Is there any way I can get better at helping her?"

"There is a book that I think would be a good first step. Although there have been many books written about borderline characteristics and how to best handle the situation, <u>Stop Walking on Eggshells</u> could have been written with you in mind. It is an apropos title because people involved with a borderline are constantly 'walking on eggshells' to avoid conflict with that person. Borderlines frequently misinterpret others' motivations and actions, while are themselves unpredictable and unable to think clearly. If you read it, you will be able to have a better understanding of your relationship with her."

Catherine enters the book title into her cell phone. "What else do you think would be helpful?"

"As I said before, first determine if she wants to be helped. There are several forms of treatment that have been developed, such as DBT - Dialectical Behavior Therapy- developed by a woman who herself was borderline. She used psychodynamic therapy and cognitive-behavioral therapy as well as Buddhist meditation ideas and blended them together into a new format. One of the main concepts of DBT is to do the opposite of whatever your impulse is. This same theory may be applied to you as well…whenever you feel like intervening, don't…as hard as that is for you. Another form of therapy is called 'mentalization,' developed by British psychologists. Here, several dimensions are analyzed to determine on which end the borderline lies: The first one deals with understanding yourself and others better; the second works on acting with more thoughtfulness instead of a typical knee-jerk reaction; the third focuses on thinking more, not only responding emotionally. This particular regimen would take time though and would require her wanting the help."

Now Catherine asks Sarah the question she had been expecting – and dreading:

"Since you said we were both fixers, I have to ask if you ever experienced what I did in your childhood."

My thoughts were wrenched back into those years again. I saw my mother before me, raging at me with ugly words. Her actions made me react without thinking, even though I knew what I was doing would cause me even more pain. As I grew, I became more independent - I retaliated by giving as good as she gave — horrible words I could never take back. And then, her curling up in a protective ball just to end what she had started. I had become the bad one in everyone's eyes, including my own. I deserved all of the punishments that were doled out to me. Even after all those years of therapy, the hurt and doubt can still waft over me, triggered by a patient's revelations.

Sarah willfully skims over the gory details and simply answers,

"Yes, I was a prime example of introjective identification. In fact, I eventually became a borderline too — just as my mother had been — and needed many years of therapy to overcome my internalized issues."

Catherine looks astonished, but convinced:

"Now I really hear what you have been saying here and in group. You realized you had to change yourself and you did. You show no signs of being like my daughter-in-law at all though. I guess therapy worked for you."

Sarah smiles but reproaches herself, thinking if Catherine only knew what she had dredged up in Sarah's thoughts just a short time ago:

"Well, who knows? Everyone still has issues. No one is perfect, but we have to acknowledge our flaws and try to reduce them. I will see you in group next week."

My voice sounded a tad too perky…had Catherine noticed? She had piercing eyes so she may well have seen through my glib veneer. There were instances where she reminded me of my mother who knew me all too well. I could sometimes fool my doting father who gave me the benefit of the doubt, perhaps because of those private sessions within the confines of his study… but not my doubting mother who never believed a word I said — probably because she was convinced of my wickedness before I was even born.

Another session has ended, but my journey is obviously still an ongoing one. How would my next patient's experiences echo within me? Have I taken on too much? Oh, Diane, why did you have to die on me??? Maria, please forgive me for I knew not what I did to you!

CHAPTER 6

PAUL THE KNIGHT-IN-ARMS

Sarah was thrilled to see Paul had opted for individual sessions, especially since she had feared that he had been put off by that first group experience. Even though he appeared to have been at ease at the time, Sarah often found that some patients are reluctant to venture further. She was also optimistic about the outcome of their efforts together. Her inner sense told her that Paul would be one of the most open among the group, not only in his revelations, but also in his acceptance of new directions she could offer him. She also found him incredibly attractive…

At that first session, he strode in confidently, a handsome black man in his mid-forties, who is both sensitive and engaging. Sarah knew he was also a psychologist, that he had been married for a few years, and that he had one daughter. She also knew that he was in a relationship with another man, but that he felt very unsure of the future of their relationship. Sarah looks at him expectantly, and his first words are direct and honest:

"I can't make up my mind about which way I want to go — gay or heterosexual. Remember what you said in group the other day about lots of men having both sexualities, in other words they are bi-sexual. Well, I've worked with some clients that are sexually confused, but I never came across that concept before. Please expand upon it."

Sarah measured her words carefully since she was speaking to him as both a colleague and a patient and she did not want to confuse the two:

"Sure… I've had lots of clients that definitely identify themselves as heterosexuals, but came into therapy because they had a dream in which they had sex with another male and were very upset by it.   In truth, they were absolutely terrified and needed some kind of professional reassurance. So, they ask if that type of fantasy means that they are secretly homosexuals. My answer is a resounding **NO**! Everyone has some desire for same sex contact at some point in their lives. Typically, women can skirt the issue without actually labeling themselves as gay. For example, women can walk holding hands, whereas men cannot. I understand what you are going through right now; you are caught in a dilemma and cannot make up your mind which way to go. So tell me what it is about men that you like."

Paul dives right in:

"Let me give you a bit of my background first. I guess it is all part of my DNA. I was never close to my dad. He was an alcoholic and not around much. My mom was a hard person to get close to because she was a harsh and unreasonable taskmaster. She needed me to take care of her, but she always criticized my every move. Nothing I did was ever right, so I've always sort of been turned off to women — not liking them first because I truly believed that a woman could never care about me. In point of fact, I was actually searching for a man to care about me — a father figure, I suppose. Now I recently found someone that I think I can make a life with. Prior to him, I was just having sex with men and sometimes with women. Even when I was married, I had little flings with men on the side…the way some men go into bathrooms and have a bit of sex, and then go home to their wives. But I always felt guilty — like

I was cheating on her. What disturbs me now is that the guy I'm with is very effeminate. Sometimes he even puts on a nightgown. I don't think he's transgender. I'm attracted to him both physically and emotionally. He's kind of a caretaker type. Do you think it's all too strange?"

In order to make him feel more comfortable, Sarah decides to use situations and terms with which he would be familiar as a trained psychologist:

"Who knows what causes a person's sexual desire? As children, we all have crushes on certain people-sometimes the same sex and sometimes the other. We play all kinds of kid games exploring the other's genitals - Playing doctor, for example. Boys often play the game of who can pee further so they can see and compare each other's penises. No one knows what causes a person's sexuality —genes, family, culture, experiences — and there are many theories. I am certain you are familiar with the 1950's and 60's research by Masters and Johnson that determined that we are all on a sexual continuum. Some are more to one side than the other and others are in the middle. Some of us want sex with both sexes, while others are on the heterosexual side. However, every once in a while they go towards the middle of the continuum. They always have a reason for it, or what I would call a rationalization, such as being in prison, needing sex, and thus having sex with another inmate.   Everyone is entitled to be attracted to a penis, wanting to be entered either orally or anally. At that point, the male is taking on the submissive role some of the time, but at other times wanting to be in control and thereby reversing the sexual roles."

I hope Paul doesn't sense how attracted I am to him. All this sex talk only makes me more drawn to him — his muscular legs, chiseled jawline, exceedingly broad shoulders and narrow waistline-he could have been one of Michelangelo's masterpieces — except he was here in the flesh, sitting so close to me that our knees were almost touching. Did he sit that way on purpose? Is he testing his manhood or just flirting to see if he can get a rise out of me?

Sarah remains aroused, but keeps her voice steady:

"I once had a female patient who was married for thirty years, had three kids, but was always having affairs with other females. She never left her husband until he discovered what had been happening, and only then did she decide she was gay."

Sarah begins to fantasize: Stella crouches before me, like a tiger waiting to pounce. Her eyes seem to swallow me, piece by piece. She is not entirely naked — just a black silky thong that snugly embraces her vagina and anus. She snaps it, holding back a corner to reveal what is beneath it. As I bend towards her, she pulls me down towards her Brazilian-waxed vagina and I lick her voraciously...she tastes like truffles. I watch as she comes, her ecstasy soaring in waves of utter passion; then it is my turn. She overpowers me with her lust, forcing my legs apart while she straps on a dildo the color of jungle vines, sinewy and thick. As she enters me, I feel as if no dildo exists — just Stella crashing against me with a throbbing intensity. I never want it to end — she is perfection. She seems to instinctively know this because just as she brings me to the absolute brink of orgasm, she withdraws just enough to persuade an even deeper response from me. While I breathlessly come, she revels in her conquest, but then punishes me by placing me on my knees before her. As she grasps my buttocks in a firm grip, she slaps them with her open palm, and then savagely sodomizes me with a stiff object that is hidden from my view. I strain to escape, but that only fuels her enjoyment. Her gusto is reaching full-pitch...I frantically seek help and then I see Paul.

Sarah shakes away the disturbing images by recalling what she had been telling Paul before her fantasies once again intruded on her reality:

"But I think she was actually bi-sexual because whenever she met a man with whom she could fall in love, she'd want to have sex with him as well. Another female patient was involved with a guy who liked transgender males so she came up with the idea of purchasing a dildo, which she wore and inserted into her boy-friend's anus, and that satisfied him. He liked being entered. Everyone is entitled to want to be entered so she pleased him in this way, and he gave up on looking for other men. The main thing is to accept who you are at this moment, and not try to decide 'What am I?' Situations can and often change. In two years you may meet a woman with whom you want to make love. Who knows what the future will hold, but your acceptance of where you are now is crucial to your well-being. Right now you are interested in this male partner, so stop labeling yourself —labeling makes you put yourself in a box — 'I'm this or that' — and it does you no good. You do not have to squeeze yourself into that box. You can be more flexible and accept that you have different choices at different times in your life."

Like me, for example! Pictures of the two of us taking turns sexually are now flashing before me. Paul inside me…me watching him writhe with pleasure as I repeatedly thrust a dildo into him. The pleasure was almost unbearable — much like it was with Walter, my former therapist who took me in hand at a younger age. In retrospect, I realize that Walter had gone well beyond moral and ethical therapy boundaries by taking advantage of his power over me just as my uncle Frank had done, yet I could not resist indulging myself with these long-lost images of Walter's technique. Much as Stella performed in my recent fantasy, Walter knew exactly what moves would bring me just to the threshold of orgasm, over and over again, before allowing me to release the passions he had instilled inside me. Paul could replace my long-lost Walter-I just knew it. But how to make the first move — with a man who professes to be gay?

Sarah meets Paul's eyes; he smiles broadly back at her…as if he had read her last thought:

"I like to be looked at as a catch by another man — chased after, rather than doing the chasing. I was often told how cute I was when I was younger… but now I'm forty-five years old and not the cute one anymore."

Sarah cannot help but be coy with him. She knows he is fishing for a compliment (*or maybe he's flirting with me*):

"You are still very attractive. Look in the mirror and say 'I'm attractive enough.' Narcissism means you need to be told by others that you are attractive or smart or anything positive, but it's you who has to believe and understand that you are good enough, and accept that everyone has male and female characteristics as defined by culture. Some of these traits are considered male and others female, but the real goal is to be androgynous, i.e., having both male and female characteristics. It's just societal mores that proclaim that males have to be this way and females another — a male who likes to cook-does that make him feminine? A woman can love to mow the lawn — does that make her male?"

Sarah then addresses Paul the Psychologist:

"Did you ever 'cure' a homosexual? The answer is that there is nothing to cure. Over the years many techniques have been developed to 'cure' homosexuality: for example, shocking the patient as he watches males having sex to strip away the desire and the impulse. It doesn't work; no one has found a way to change sexual orientation, which begins very early in life. When did you first realize that you were not only attracted to girls, but to boys as well?"

Paul grimaces:

"I was very young — about eight— or so — and I felt terrible like there was something seriously wrong with me. So I kept forcing myself to go with girls…I was all mixed up."

Paul towers above Stella and me — is he my knight in shining armor, there to rescue me? His expression gives nothing away, but his next move does. He lies down next to me, ramming his tongue into my mouth. Stella continues her flagellations, with Paul as her more-than-willing partner. They take turns by reversing their positions, but Paul also presses his penis into my vagina – I am at their mercy…and I like it! Once again, I am out of control in a sexual situation. Why does the very idea bring me so much pleasure? As they continue their profane ministrations upon me, I lose myself in the moment, satisfied to surrender wholly to them.

The office walls encroach upon her last desire. Although this time she is more unwilling to relinquish those gratifying images that engulfed her, Sarah chooses to toss a new scenario into Paul's session: *(I can't believe I'm telling him about this — am I being just a bit too forward here?):*

"I had a patient years ago who became so close to me emotionally, sharing his thoughts and feelings like he never had in his life before — and so he began to want to date women, transferring his feelings for me as his therapist onto women at large. He tried for a while, but ended up with a male partner. Dating women was okay for him, but he still preferred males - So it is whomever you prefer that counts — not what society or family or friends tell you that you should be."

Paul looks at her searchingly. *(Is he taking the bait?)*

"I had heard that you had taught human sexuality at a university — is that correct? Is that where you honed your skills on this topic?"

Actually it was my life experiences that made me an expert on that particular topic, but I can't share that thought with him — at least not now.

Sarah hides a smile:

"Well, it's interesting that you brought that up. When I taught, I also showed films to my classes — not hard porn — just ones about older people having fun in the bedroom, or two men or two women and a man, etc. The male students loved to watch the two women making love, and they also thought men's penetrating each other was just fine. The only thing that bothered most of them was when the two men kissed each other. For some reason, those scenes turned them off."

Sarah looks up at Paul to see if he had any reaction. Seeing nothing obvious on his face or in his body language (his knees were still almost caressing hers), she goes on:

"I probed *(good innuendo!)* further, conducting private surveys after the movies. Nobody – men or women — was upset when one male put his penis into the other, but everyone got upset when the men kissed — but never when the women did. I once interviewed a prostitute. She told me she exchanged sex for money, but never kissed the man. Kissing somehow indicates a relationship. That was what the men were objecting to. Perhaps for you now, it may be that you can have sex with a guy, but you cannot accept the idea of having a true relationship with a male. The very concept may make you uptight because you grew up in this culture. I once had a homosexual come talk to the class about his childhood, and when he first realized he had desires for other males. As a child, he saw how the gay population was unacceptable to society, which caused him so much pain that he kept his homosexuality a secret for years. Paul, you have adopted that viewpoint as well and so part of you now finds that that part of you — the interest in other men — is unacceptable. Although society is improving its attitude towards homosexuals, we know it still isn't completely there yet."

Sarah presents a further example as clarification:

"There was a Pakistani girl who was on TV recently. Do you remember what I said in group about how I wanted to be one of the boys? Well, so did she! She wanted the freedom to play soccer and other so-called boy sports, but girls were not allowed to join teams in her country. So she disguised herself as a boy — not meaning that she wanted a penis — the classic Freudian 'penis envy.' She just wanted to play a simple game of soccer. She became a great player, but the religious leaders condemned her actions and she had to go back to being a girl again. She said she spent half of her life as a girl and half as a boy, but now she's just being 'her.' She wrote a book about her experiences growing up in Pakistan as a girl and all of the religious and cultural taboos. There will always be conflict between what you can do as a boy and what you can do as a girl, including the different sexual roles. The benefits of being male, even in America, still exist. No one has definitively cracked that glass ceiling-not just yet. Your sexuality is not a disease or a deficit; it is simply a difference that people grow into, and no one can determine how it evolves. Psychologists and religious clerics have tried to change one's sexual leanings through various experiments amounting to torture, but they have never succeeded."

Sarah believed they had begun important work in this session, but now it was time to end it. She promised to address his feelings of loss the next time they met. However, the erotic urges Paul had awakened in her were deeply disturbing. She had been convinced that she had successfully expunged Walter from her psyche many years ago, but now here he was back in her thoughts like an erratic/erotic boomerang! He had not been her first lover, but he had introduced her to what could only be described as delight verging on deviance.

As she watched Paul leave, deep in thought, Sarah indulged herself in a few of her own…

I had always wanted to be one of the boys, and back then boys had a lot more freedom — in their choice of careers, their sexual experiences, and in so many other areas. Men had no problem having both a family and a career — no need to juggle the two. Boys could have it all…I was intrigued by this power from a very young age so I would engage in innocent sexual acts with them, never going all the way… Two boys fondle my breasts, each vying for a turn, and then both of them touching me at once. Their eyes rove over my body as I masturbate until I almost reach climax. They cannot stop themselves from coming all over their cleaned and ironed pants…how would they explain the stains to their moms? I turned the tables here – I commanded them! My favorite fantasies always involved more than one lover at a time…a minimum of two, but sometimes as many as four — all working on me, my mouth, my vagina, my breasts, my anus, (including my rear end…my go-to erogenous zone!) This is how to be the master/mistress of my domain. If guys could do it, why not me?

In later years, I was at times confused about my leanings. I remember that I actually had a crush on another counselor at a camp in Maine when I was seventeen or so, and not understanding what it meant. Was I gay? I can still see her supple breasts, rounded butt, and tanned physique-she was just so beautiful — hard, yet soft at the same time. I was intrigued, but never acted on my secret infatuation with her. I often wondered if she felt the same towards me…her body's fragrance-a blend of baby oil and berries — wafts over me from time to time…and it still brings a flush to my cheeks. Stella reminds me of her — she could be a sweetly generous lover, but then turn harsh without any warning. Is it that dual nature that lures me to her…the way my loving father coaxed me into submission with his spankings and his kindnesses afterwards?

As an adult, I finally acted on my impulses: I first experimented by having sex with another woman and a man. When I saw how much the man liked watching us two women make love, I really got into it. By then, I understood that everyone can be attracted to both sexes without being "homosexual." It took me a while to fully grasp and accept that concept. In general, I preferred sex with men; in fact, I never just had sex with a woman alone-except one time when we were waiting for the man to show up, so we started before he came into the room. As I recall, it was lovely. She tasted like honey — sweet and warm — and her movements were graceful. We moved in sync with one another, anticipating what each of us wanted in such a natural way. Our climax was simultaneous — two bodies in sheer ecstasy — a slow, rhythmic pas-de-deux between two equal partners.

Perhaps Paul would enjoy having sex with his gay lover while I watched. I could have sex with another man at the same time, and then — switch partners! I am so attracted to him; for me, he has it all — the whole package — looks, intelligence, character, and sex appeal. I want to hold onto him — how can I do that when he has told me from the start that he's gay? Mixed couples may be the solution. I have already engaged in sex with two men, and really took pleasure in seeing the two of them make out with each other. I was turned on like never before. They were both heterosexuals, but once in a while they enjoyed being with another man. YET, in order to make the experience more acceptable, they had to have a woman present… the classic ménage-à-trois. One had been sexually abused as a child several times and that experience made him afraid that he was homosexual since he achieved orgasms with his abuser. I think that confuses any child who was sexually abused by a same-sex person. He asks himself, "Why am I getting turned on?" They do not understand that their body is simply responding to the physical stimulation, and not the idea that it is the same-sex person touching their penis…I must remember to question Paul about his childhood at our next session — he mentioned a father, but just barely. Why? Perhaps the subject was too sensitive for him to revisit.

In spite of herself, Sarah could not help returning to the images that had given her pause during the session…she begins to fantasize anew, but this time sans Stella:

Paul stood up from his chair — there was no denying his intent. His dark eyes surveyed her body slowly and deliberately, as if to determine which area to start with first. His large hands enclosed her breast; he squeezed it hard — just the way Sarah liked it. Then he turned his attention to the other one, methodically unbuttoning first her blouse, and then her bra — snap! His tongue was rough against her tender skin, but Sarah didn't mind. He still hadn't kissed her-was he remembering what she had said about the prostitute? Was this his way of silently communicating to her that this was just a one-time indulgence? Without realizing it, Sarah saw her panties had been wrapped around her ankles — a silky chain that was surprisingly strong. As Paul opened her up, he spread her across his lap so that her backside was there for the taking. He smacked it, then caressed it, slapped it, then tasted it…she was more of a passive participant here. He wanted no interaction with her…Then, he quickly turned her over across the tiny desk and there she laid, a supine supplicant, begging for more of the same. He satisfied her wishes several times, holding her fast in his grasp, not allowing her to squirm free. It was strangely liberating, not being given any choice about what was happening to her. Her orgasm was absolute and pure; she felt like an untouched virgin in his hands. This was the way the "First Time" should have been. Paul had taken things in hand, but his touch was gentle, not coarse or violent as that rough-and-tumble encounter had been in the car so long ago. Maybe things would have been different with me — no abortions, no Walter, no abusive marriages…I'll never know for sure, but I must finish what was started in therapy before I can truly help my patients.

In short, while Sarah felt helpless in his hands, she also recognized at once that Paul was indeed her knight in shining armor because he had given her back her sense of control over her own life. By giving in to her sexual fantasy, Sarah felt alive again. She was no longer imprisoned by Shame and Guilt, the two guards her parents had secured to keep her in her place. She was now aware that a new road map had to be charted for her journey. Joy of joys!

Sarah could now openly embrace her erotic reveries…Paul's session had aroused an integral part of who she was, calling to the forefront the shades of herself that lingered still yet within her hidden self…shadows that definitively defined Sarah, past-present-and future.

CHAPTER 7

GEORGE THE FIXER

George shuffles in, casually dressed in a navy blue knit cable sweater and khaki chinos. He reminds Sarah of a sea captain set adrift by a mutinous crew. He is struggling to hold on to his position of strength, but seems on the verge of capsizing into the dark swirling sea that had become his world. He is looking for a lifeline — seeking control here, something he did not have in his everyday life. So his first question is more of a challenge, much like a teacher's to a student:

"I told you a bit about my trouble with my son in the group session. Do you remember what I said?"

Sarah jumps in, following his succinct style:

"Yes, you told me that your son is thirty; you described him as a *user* who is causing you a lot of pain." Having answered him, Sarah quickly takes charge of the session: "Now let's explore your relationship with him. First, describe him to me."

George thought a while before giving his answer,

"He can be a real charmer-when he was young he was an attractive man. His features were handsome, never cute-even as a child. He always had boldness about him, like he was King of the World! To tell you the truth, he frightens me a bit...to the point of my being unable to refuse him anything he asks. His manner makes some people label him a sociopath, but he's really not a terrible person. He just knows how to manipulate people, especially me. He's always figuring out ways to get me to give him money."

My mother was the same way…as I got older, she would use the same methodology she used on my father to get money out of me. She would plead with me like a spoiled child — wheedling and then becoming more irate if I hesitated to give her what she wanted. She took on the cloak of entitlement — "I'm the one who gave you your life, gave you a roof over your head and food to eat, you owe it to me!" I felt like an ingrate for many years afterwards, but at the same time, I also suspected that I was a real chump! George is in a similar spot, but this time the roles are reversed — a spoiled child demanding what he believes to be his birthright from a father who only wants his son to love him…

George goes on with his description, almost as if he could read Sarah's recent thoughts:

"He's constantly coming up with one scheme or another to start a new venture, and I always am there to help him follow his dream. I think or hope that this time he'll finally succeed — but he never does. Maybe that's why he uses drugs and lies to everyone all the time. I suppose I'm just making excuses for him because I can't face the truth. Diane told me I was an enabler. Do you agree with her diagnosis of me?"

Sarah could see he was becoming upset and aggravated with the situation, but still hopeful so she continues further:

"I don't know if enabler is the right term. Many different words come to mind. I call myself a fixer but my friend calls me a meddler. As parents, we are always trying to fix our kids, but what we don't realize is that any real correction only occurs before the age of about seven. By that time, their personality is pretty much formed. Tell me more about how he behaved as a young child."

George's face takes on a painful expression…

"He was always cold and distant towards his mother and me, as well as his sister. On the advice of a school administrator, we took him for testing to a psychologist when he was about nine years old. The test results were interpreted by a therapist, who used the term 'manipulator' in his final analysis. The irony is that my son now says that I am the manipulator in our relationship! He often tells me that the only reason I give in to his demands is to get him to do what I want. He accuses me of trying to control him."

Sarah muses aloud,

"I guess we all are manipulators in our own way because we all try to change the other person. What I've learned over the years is that the only one you can truly change is *you*, and even that is very tough to do. It requires years of work and self-reflection in therapy sessions just like this one. I am finally learning not to even ask my children any questions about themselves. Instead, I allow them to decide what they want to share with me about their lives because as soon as I begin any inquiry, they make me feel like an intruder. In fact, just to avoid any confrontation with me, they often feel compelled to lie if they are doing something that they know would anger me — just like your son. You are putting him on the spot when you delve too deeply. You probably already know much too much about his life...but only the version he cares to share with you. Give me an example of how he uses you."

George seemed eager to share this particular story, either out of desperation, weariness, or both:

"He wants to buy used cars and resell them so I gave him $50,000 as a 'loan,' but his past history makes me doubt that he will ever pay me back. Afterwards, he becomes very angry with me, accusing me of never doing anything for him. I am baffled and frustrated by this ongoing situation! No matter how much I have done for him in the past, it is never enough for him in the present. It's all forgotten...He doesn't even show any concern or appreciation for me or our family."

Sarah explains,

"It's called 'biting the hand that feeds you.' Paradoxically, there's a great deal of resentment built up when a grown child keeps needing and receiving from a parent. The two (parent and child) become what is called codependents. In your case, it looks like he's the dependent one; but in point of fact, you need him to need you. This coming-to-the-rescue scenario makes you feel like a good parent or the stronger one in the relationship, but there are always expectations that arise on your part and he, in a passive-aggressive way, will not give you what you want. His aggressive behavior towards you — even after you comply with his demand — is self-defeating, but he can't help it. He is trying to regain the control he thinks he has lost, but in actuality never had. On your part, you continue to believe that this time your generosity will work, but you know you are fooling yourself. You need to examine why you have to be the perfect loving father. When your son needs something from you, do his demands make you feel important to him?"

George shakes his head.

"I never viewed our relationship in that way. I always fear that I will abandon him out of sheer disgust, but he is the one abandoning me. He shows no concern for my well-being. The only emotion I get from him is a burning resentment."

Sarah could see tears shimmering in his sad eyes. She knew she just had to fix him somehow!

"Do you go to Al-Anon? I strongly suggest you and your wife attend a meeting there. Their basic message is that the person you have to take care of is yourself. Do not think of it as being selfish. You need to strengthen yourself for your son's sake."

As George contemplated her words, Sarah continues,

"What I mean is that you have to survive in order to be there for your loved ones. When you suffer, it is impossible to accomplish anything good for either yourself or your son. You must learn to accept that you can never change him. He alone is the one who should decide to stop self-medicating himself with alcohol and drugs. Think about the fact that an addict needs to first hit bottom before he can ascend from the place in which he has put himself. Everyone has his own bottom; some addicts are able to continue their self-defeating spiral for years in pain and agony before they decide to find help. In my opinion, Alcoholics Anonymous or Narcotics Anonymous is the best choice for lifelong rehabilitation, but only after on-site help has succeeded in not only eliminating the drugs, but also lowering the desire for them from the body and mind. The motivation must start with the addict; no matter how much you as his father insist that he seek treatment for his habit, he will never listen."

George then goes to the core of his concern by asking her,

"Is my son emotionally disturbed? Would you say he is a sociopath, as others have indicated to me?"

"Everyone has personality issues. I've had them my entire life and have been in therapy off and on for thirty years to address them. I was a fixer even as a child. I tried to counsel my parents because they were always fighting with each other. That is probably one of the reasons why I studied psychology as a student; I wanted to be a therapist. I came to the realization early on that the only way I could truly help anyone would be when they came to me for professional therapy instead of voicing my amateur opinions to my friends and family. Blindly offering advice, whether it is solicited or unsolicited, is not the best solution."

To tell the truth, the only time my parents fought with one another was over me. I just loved the attention because then I was in control. My father was the indulgent one as well as the enforcer...he would punish me firmly and quickly — his anger subsided almost immediately. But my mother let her anger stew for days on end. She would give me that look — kind of like the evil eye — and then she would sting me with her words. Oh, she was merciless. When she saw my father was teetering over to her side, she would increase her assaults…but I was ready for her. Experience taught me to wait for just the right moment to insert a wicked wedge between them. I pretended to be the peacemaker, knowing full well that my father would come to my defense, while my mother doubled down on her offense. Am I telling George the whole story here? Was my motivation as selfless as I am making it out to be by calling myself the fixer? Did I really want to fix the situation or inflame it so that I could feel my father's love for me? I would be the Conqueror; I would be in control now.

George had ignored Sarah's lack of attention…he was used to being ignored. To bring her back to him, he asks her another direct question:

"So what advice would you give me?"

Coming back with a jolt, Sarah resumes her role as therapist by firmly reiterating what she had been telling him,

"I don't really want to be put in the position of advisor here, except about where to go for supplemental support such as Al-Anon. During our sessions, my goal is to help you learn more about your own self and others. It is called 'mentalization' — some of us are experts at reading ourselves, but we may not be as good at reading others. Your son is good at reading you, but probably not all that great at reading himself since he doesn't know what motivates him to so completely destroy his life. As I said before, he has to want to change or learn more about himself before he can even begin to heal. The same goes for you, although you are not an alcoholic or addict. However, you cannot control your impulses when it comes to your son, in the same way that he cannot curb his addictions. What I am attempting to do here is to get you to look deeper into what is behind your determination to fix your son despite all the failures through all of these years. Any ideas as to why you continue on in what you know to be a hopeless cause and journey?"

George grins back at her knowingly:

"Actually, when you said you tried to fix your parents when you were a child (Hearing his words, Sarah involuntarily flinches.)…

well, it reminded me of my own experiences and reactions, not just with my parents… my dad was a secret drinker, never wanting to admit that he was an alcoholic … but also towards my siblings. My brother was an addict and my sister had emotional difficulties. She's been institutionalized for many years. Despite my good intentions, I was never able to help her or my brother, and now I find myself going through the same motions with my son. I suppose I never get it. I just keep thinking this time it will work. Duh!! Pretty stupid isn't it?"

It was the same with my father – I could always smell the alcohol on his breath, even though he tried camouflaging it with peppermint candy. The claret he consumed during those spanking rituals was just the tip of the iceberg. From there, he advanced on to the hard stuff – Dewars was his go-to liquor. He kept several bottles in his study, but never drank it in public. He was The Great Pretender; strange to admit, but I just realized that now.

This last revelation almost sidetracks the session, until Sarah instinctively rushes back to protest his last remark:

"I would not call it stupid; it's a learned pattern of behavior that you've done all your life and one you have internalized. It's very hard to shift internalized behavior because you are used to always being concerned about others — it is actually a trained reflex — and not enough about yourself and how to make yourself happy. You are terribly unhappy now over your son. I completely understand, but it is time to start caring about you! Don't think of it as being self-centered, even though your internal self will name you as one every step of the way. Think of it as being the only way to survive. Remember we all have but one life. I know it's been said so many times before — in greeting cards, on posters, even by preachers — 'You Need to Help Yourself before You Can Help Others.' Believe me… it's worth repeating because so many of us balk at the very idea of it."

George counters with:

"But I always feel like a selfish person. My parents were always telling me that I was selfish, maybe because I was the most normal one in the family, which is not saying much considering my family! So I find myself always trying not to be selfish. I drive myself to keep being helpful to others, like going on errands for my spoiled mother-in-law or shoveling snow for my nosy neighbors, yet I cannot stop feeling selfish and guilty…I want to find out why."

Sarah attempts to redirect the conversation:

"Let's return to the concept of internalization. We all encompass the image that our parents had of us and it is a real struggle to change it because it is an identity given to us early in life, embedded in our brains, so to speak. It is natural for us to fear relinquishing or even moderating that image because we don't know what image will replace it. We have trouble casting aside our parents' views of us because those judgments, good and bad, keep us connected to them. That is one of the ways therapy can help a person: The therapist holds up a metaphorical mirror and tries to present you with a picture of yourself that incorporates more than that which you grew up thinking about yourself. I had a patient once whose mother's criticism of her was so intense that she continued denouncing herself even after her mother had died. The bad seed that her mother had sown stubbornly remained with her. I am pleased to report that after a number of years with me, she was able to eradicate that image bestowed upon her as an insufficient and worthless daughter. I figuratively engaged in hand-to-hand combat with her mother's ghost, and I emerged victorious!"

How ironic is it that I am able to show my patients their true selves using that invisible mirror, but am unable to look at myself in it? Have I been fooling everyone here? Am I really as intact as I claim to be? Sure, I talk as if I can fix whatever ails them, but can I really do as I say? Be that as it may, I only know that the mirror of truth is failing me…but maybe I can at least help George see his inner reflection.

Sarah shrugs away her self-doubts in order to concentrate on George now:

"I always say it like I see it. So, it is my intention to hold up that same mirror for you. I see you as a caring, loving person… I would suggest you look in the mirror and repeat to yourself 'I am good enough.' Take a good look at yourself: You are coming to therapy to learn about yourself. That is an important first step. Be proud that you want to change even though you realize that the journey you are undertaking will be brutally painful at times. I will accompany you, sometimes leading, but often following your lead. Do you understand what I have been trying to get across to you? I need to know."

The sad-eyed man looks directly into Sarah's eyes. She felt he was looking into her own history. He was a kind and sympathetic fellow traveler. He then ruefully admits to her what he has been slowly realizing:

"Yes, but, it's difficult to take it in completely. I guess that's why therapy takes time."

Sarah adds, "… and effort."

Continuing, Sarah ends the session with,

"I will see you in group next week. Carefully consider and review our session before we next meet. It's only your thinking that can help you change your behavior. You cannot allow only your emotions to run your life. Thoughts and emotions have to combine…that is what leads to wisdom. Everyone needs that type of balance. Some people are either very emotional or very intellectualized. The middle and best ground in life is wisdom, which translates into your using both sides of your brain — not just one or the other. One more crucial caveat for you: Guilt is a useless emotion. We all feel guilty at one time or another, but that reaction cannot change what we have done. The past is the past and the future is unknown so worrying about the future certainly will not change the future. We are only causing harmful anxiety by attempting to control our lives remotely."

George leaves her office, looking slightly more cheerful than before, but not all that much. The furrows remained on his forehead and his walk was still more of a shuffle than a stride, but at least he was not as bent over as he had been earlier. Sarah hoped she had eased some of the burdens a little. Then she could hear him whistling a little ditty — she could swear she heard a sea chanty and smiled.

Perhaps I'm wrong in my self-analysis – I'm damn good at what I do in here so who cares why I went into this field in the first place??? It makes a good story to tell my patients…and me!

Sarah leaves the session, temporarily satisfied with her justification, yet still feeling a bit uneasy about her own unraveling, which has continued to chase her throughout each and every individual session with the patients in Diane's group. She reflects further into the evening, when the night shades create deepening shadows of suspicion.

George has triggered such turmoil inside of me — while it is true that he appeared happier after the session than he was before it – I, on the other hand, am becoming increasingly skeptical about my capabilities as a therapist, my reasons for becoming one, and indeed my own state-of mind. Hadassah is destined to become my trial-by-fire…that is — if she actually shows up!

CHAPTER 8

HADASSAH THE WRETCH

Hadassah came into her first individual session looking even more downhearted than in group…her bloodshot eyes swimming in sadness. Tears seemed to have diluted their color into a washed-out blue, like jeans that had been faded by a combination of sun and chlorine.

Her manner was so dejected that Sarah felt compelled to ask her what was wrong. Her voice was desultory, yet Sarah felt a deep-seated resentment lurking in the shadows, possibly against her and probably against the entire world:

"Nothing, I just feel this way all the time… all my life, day and night, winter, summer, spring, and fall. As I told you in group *(Sarah could hear the unspoken accusation-weren't you listening to me, Sarah???)*, my parents would never allow me to enjoy life. Joy was an unnatural emotion in my house. If I dared to plan an outing with friends to give me a chance to escape the doom-and-gloom that lingered in the rooms like the stink of rotten milk, they would find some task I simply had to complete on that very day. I always had to follow their strict orders, even though I moved out of their house in my twenties. But that was just a physical separation. I tried eliminating them from my mind by not visiting them on a regular basis —

only when their phone calls and guilt trips became unbearable! They finally died and I thought 'peace at last,' but no-o-o-o…their voices still whine at me and I haven't been able to silence them, even after five years of therapy. I have been treated by a number of different therapists unsuccessfully until Diane - and now I've lost her!"

Hadassah's voice had transitioned to what could best be described as a wail, expanding and filling the room until it became almost difficult to breathe. Her pain and misery were infectious, weakening Sarah like a feverish disease. Struggling to overcome a strange sensation of nausea, Sarah dutifully doffs her therapy hat:

"Diane's death is understandably painful. I get it. Here you were, finally getting somewhere and then she abandoned you. Do you feel any anger towards her like some of the others in the group? Even though it seems unfair to blame Diane for dying, it's still a feeling that has legitimacy."

Hadassah's eyes are accusing and scolding. "What's wrong with you? I know Diane couldn't help herself. She's gone…the very idea of your trying to blame poor Diane for my agony! Typical psycho mumbo-jumbo! I am not angry with her (her voice rising to a snarling bark). I am realizing that I am now left alone here on this earth, just like my infuriating parents had always predicted and secretly hoped for me!"

Sarah uneasily waits for her to continue, although she instinctively knew her story as well as she knew her own.

She narrates her history in a monotone, as if she were repeating a well-worn tale:

"Everyone else in my parents' family, except my father's mother, had died in the Holocaust, but even she had suffered horribly in Auschwitz. My God, how they reveled in repeating those nightmarish details about decomposing corpses, babies slaughtered at birth, brutal rapes, starvation to such a degree that sons took the moldy bread away from their own fathers — oh, the inhumanity mixed together with their own survivor guilt! I truly believe that I was nurtured on it from my very conception. I call it the placenta of guilt. You see, both my parents had been sent to Denmark before the Nazis started their own Reign of Terror in Germany. Then they managed to procure visas to England, and then America. Instead of being thrilled to be alive, they were miserable their whole lives and felt unworthy of life itself. They never felt happy about surviving — nor did my paternal grandmother - I guess because her husband, her parents, her sisters and brothers, and her other children all died either in concentration camps or they were just shot in cold blood on the streets. My mother's parents, her sister, and her aunts and uncles also perished, leaving her even more isolated than my father. I felt she should have felt joy — giving birth to a child in a new land — a fresh start, so to speak."

Sarah interrupts her, "I'm sure you are aware of survivor's guilt...you used the term just now."

Hadassah's eyes flash back at her, no longer tearful, but filled with resentment:

"Yes, but so what! Can't you understand that they made my life miserable — always judging me and demanding that I be a better student? I got A's in high school, but they wanted perfect scores down the line — a perfect child for imperfect parents! I was NEVER good enough for them. I tried for a while, but then I gave up..."

Once again, Sarah finds herself interjecting her own feelings into the conversation, even though her instincts tell her to refrain from them with this patient; the compulsion to do so is too strong to resist:

"I know exactly what you mean. My parents also miraculously escaped the Holocaust, but never rejoiced in it. They passed that gene onto me too. If I got 98, my father said why not 100, and soon that mark was not only never good enough for him, but for me as well. He was a bitter and depressed man, well aware of his own shortcomings. Since he never finished high school, he yearned for me to be successful, validating his existence. He demanded that I obtain a Ph.D. - which I did. He also drank a great deal of alcohol, which I believe now was his way of medicating himself. At times he was physically abusive when drunk, but my mother never even tried to protect me. She was just submissive to him and always very angry with me. The only way I could escape their physical and emotional abuse was to go in my room and study, study, study!"

Hadassah appears bored and a bit indignant about Sarah's monologue. Realizing she may have gone on too long, Sarah turns the conversation back towards Hadassah by asking, "What did you do to escape?"

Hadassah continues in a tone that was even cooler towards Sarah than before:

"I just dropped out of college and moved to another city to put some physical distance between us. It turns out I was my own worst enemy because then I was forced to take menial jobs just to survive. As you should know, if you remember what I said in group, I never married because I was unable to trust anyone. I've just been a loner for as long as I can recall. No friends, no boyfriends, not even a pet! (Here she smiled ruefully.) I was trained at a young age to always fear anyone else taking over and running my life."

After this admission, Hadassah reveals a hint of jealous curiosity. "So, Sarah, how did you manage to pull it off even though we share similar backgrounds?"

Sarah is reluctant to talk too much more about herself, given Hadassah's reactions. She keeps her answer short:

"I began going to therapy as a college student. It was offered at no charge there. Afterwards, I spent at least thirty years with seven different therapists, much like you have. I continue working on myself even now since one of my early therapists considered me a borderline personality. We can continue a discussion of what that means in our next session."

Sarah spoke the last line firmly because she could see Hadassah was worked up again. In order to end the session on a high note, she ended up by saying,

"Hadassah, you have been honest in your revelations-a trait I have always found to be the most important in the road to recovery. I look forward to seeing you in group and at a second session very soon."

I simply must end this session now. I feel the room spinning and I'm afraid I will faint dead away in front of her. Her whole being reeks of despair — something I am usually capable of banishing from the patient's spirit, but Hadassah has a powerful will, and if I let her, she will inflict tremendous damage on me. Better to break away now — and give me time to breathe before she smothers me.

Hadassah unsteadily rose from her chair. Her shoulders remained hunched over and her eyes, while not tearful, lacked any vestige of optimism. She left without speaking. Sarah usually would have noticed her patient's mood, but she was very aware that this particular patient was a true danger to her because of the dark memories she had dredged up inside of Sarah. She was reaching for that oxygen mask so that she would be able to help Hadassah the next time.

Concentration camp…why did that memory of Hadassah's bother me so much? Of course, as a Jewish woman, the very idea should be a nightmare, yet I also felt a sexual arousal as she spoke. Why?

Sarah now forced herself to confront something from a long time ago — her shameful sexual fantasy that she had conveniently forgotten had NOT been cured by her second therapist. In fact, Walter, a handsome man in his early thirties, was able to give Sarah the sexual outlet she desired at the time.

Behind his closed office doors, I described my secret fantasy to Walter – the one about being tied up like a slave girl in Auschwitz, much like my Jewish aunts might have been. The Nazi commander in his crisp black uniform ran his hands over my naked, unwashed body, and thrust his thick fingers

deeply into me. He had an evil smile, but I loved it! Then, he would whip me, calling me horrible names: Slut! Whore! These were the names my father and mother had called me over and over again. As I masturbated to this image, I became more and more excited until my guilt overwhelmed me and I stopped.

While I spoke to Walter about it, I found myself getting moist. I was embarrassed to realize that I still enjoyed this same fantasy. I turned to confess to Walter and was surprised, yet secretly pleased to see a definite bulge in his pants that had not been there before. Was he a fellow masochist?

Walter saw that I had noticed what was happening to him. He was a direct man and got straight to the point. He told me about his own childhood — how his father used to give him enemas as a punishment while his mother stood by watching him yelp helplessly and then submit. After a while, he looked forward to this unique and odd punishment because he was turned on by the whole experience. We recognized that we shared similar fetishes. Walter ended his role as my therapist then and there. He was eager to change to that of being my sexual partner in an S&M relationship…and I shared his enthusiasm.

Sarah almost swoons at the images now before her…*she and Walter taking turns spanking each other. Switching roles is just so satisfying, which is why I urged Barry and Gladys to do just that. I think they will find their bedroom activities more to their liking now — spicy and explosive. I just know that I loved thrusting those custom-designed dildos that Walter had brought along — sleek and thin…a perfect fit — hard into his anus as he moaned and wriggled. I liked being the enforcer, but was often wracked by guilt afterwards. I much preferred Walter's rough treatment of me — first a playful paddling with a hairbrush, then more of a tanning with a tiny red switch, then a whipping that stopped short of a real beating…which is when he thrust himself into all of my openings again and again.*

Sarah feels a familiar wetness in her panties.

Walter even enjoyed listening on the phone as I was being entered by another man…he would almost squeal with delight while I laughed at him. My other partner was more than willing to participate in these sex games.

Once he learned my fetish, Walter would spank me (Sarah grew wetter at the very word) *with gusto. I lost myself in between the pain and pleasure. But here I was in charge! Knowing that, in spite of being spanked, I believed I was the punisher instead of the victim because I CHOSE TO BE SPANKED. In that way, I was finally on top instead of being spread across my father's lap, helpless, yet stimulated by my prostrate position. However, I was more thrilled when I was not actually in charge, but forced into any type of sex act. Rapist truckers gang-banging a virgin hitchhiker was a favorite scenario of my own doing, not just with Walter, but with all of my lovers…I suppose it gave me an out – I was not the initiator so therefore I could feel guiltless in front of my parents' judging eyes. I was a passive body, being acted upon, beyond my control. I particularly relished the idea of being watched — even by that older man who spied on me as I masturbated on my rooftop in Brooklyn. He knew I knew he was there, and that made me excited all the more wildly. He was the offender in this situation, not me — but why did I like it so much?*

Sarah's orgasm was suddenly upon her. She was angry with herself, even though she had taken great pleasure in it. She was even angrier with Hadassah. She knew she was being unfair, but Hadassah was the catalyst in this regression. Sarah was determined not to let her patient have the reins next time.

Session 2

Appearing even more crestfallen than before, Hadassah heavily plops into her chair. She had been absent for the last two group sessions and had canceled all of her other individual sessions with Sarah. Sarah still felt a leftover resentment towards her, which was made more intense by Hadassah's absences. She had wanted to continue what was started, perhaps more for her own sake than that of her patient. Nevertheless, she was relieved to see Hadassah back again; a nagging worry had been eating at Sarah for weeks now.

Before Sarah could speak, Hadassah turns to face her: "You know, I thought you would be different from the others. Maybe because we shared names that were so traditionally Jewish…if you read your Bible, you would know that Sarah was Abraham's helpmate, a true healer in every sense of the word. I suppose I expected more from you than Diane because of your namesake. I don't know… maybe because I have reached the end of the line with you. You are my last hope, but I'm afraid you can't help me. You're too wrapped up in yourself."

Outwardly, Sarah is incensed at what she believed was an unfair assessment of her therapy skills, but inwardly, she had to admit that Hadassah was right. She had gotten lost in her own thoughts, abandoning Hadassah in that torrent of emotions that had engulfed her after their first session. She prayed she would have the opportunity to change course with her, and so she picked up where she had left off in their first and only individual session months before.

"Did Diane ever speak to you about borderline personality?"

Hadassah appears irritated, possibly because she had heard this all before.

In a weary voice, she responds, "Yes, Diane told me all about them; she labeled my mother as one."

Sarah excitedly agrees, "So was my mother! I only realized it after I became a shrink. And I probably became one because I kept trying to fix my parents, although always unsuccessfully."

Hadassah chooses to challenge that last statement by pointing out, "But you've had a pretty successful life haven't you?"

Sarah blithely continues, "Yes, I've been happy for a long while. It's been a difficult road though."

Hadassah glances quickly at Sarah, scrutinizing her more closely: "I find that hard to believe. You seem to have led a charmed life when compared to mine. You have lots of friends — even in the group! Pauline is crazy about you, but then again, she is fairly easy when it comes to trusting people — another one with no real problems — very self-absorbed if you ask me! Most of those people have no idea what it's like to be me! I'm always being criticized there — by EVERYONE…Don't you see that?"

Sarah tries to redirect her patient with a direct question: "I studied Chi Quong, a moving meditation and found it helped me. Do you ever try meditation?"

Hadassah grows aggravated: "No. My mind is always overactive. I am unable to sleep most nights because I can't turn my thoughts off."

Sarah presses on, hopeful that this discussion would give her more to work with as time went on, "What do you keep thinking about?"

"I just keep worrying about my future. I have no one who will be there for me as I grow older and older."

"Why don't you find some people to make friends with?"

Truly exasperated now, Hadassah practically screeches back, "I told you already that I've tried. No one likes me. For the life of me, I can't understand how you get people to pay you good money when you don't even try to listen to what they're saying. You always seem preoccupied- off in a world of your own! What are you day-dreaming about anyway?"

Sarah blushes, feeling guilty and embarrassed that Hadassah may have somehow witnessed her sexual adventures after their first session.

"I'm not daydreaming, Hadassah…I'm just trying to find ways to reach you so I can help you."

Hadassah murmurs under her breath, but Sarah continues:

"You believe that others don't like you because you project your own view of yourself onto others. You don't like who you are and, as a result, you cannot help feeling that others don't like you either, but you may be mistaken. How do you think I feel about you?"

Hadassah jumps at this question, thankful for the chance to shout: "I've got you now, Miss Know-It-All! You certainly don't think well of me. I'm uneducated, and you feel superior towards me because your intelligence and your strength gave you the where-withal to escape! My life is a shadow of yours, except that I never got the chance to stroll in the sun without a care in the world!"

Sarah speaks softly to diffuse Hadassah's increasing rage to-wards her," Yes, you're right about the fact that I can identify with you. We have similar original backgrounds and I can appreciate very well what you went through. We just took different paths. I was lucky in some ways because I was a rebel. For example, I would lie to my parents about where I was going when I went out."

Where is he? I can only be at the library for just so long before those two incubi become suspicious — and I don't want to be caught with my pants down — that's funny since that's exactly what's going to be going on! I caught sight of his beat-up, but snazzy convertible coming around the cor-ner. Yes, he had technically raped me that first time, but maybe I was asking for it. That's what he said to me and all his pals. I only knew I liked what he did to me so I kept on coming back for more — anything to struggle free from my parents' grip on me. Besides I loved sex with him. He was brutal, but he made me happy. He was my come-to-life fantasy! Of course, I never imagined our lust would lead to an abortion…here comes that pestering guilt-ridden regret again"

Sarah comes back to the present with a jolt. Just how long she had been lost in reverie she could not say for certain. She decides to continue her train of thought without hesitating again:

"So I was a liar and you weren't. You took on the role of the good girl until you left home, but your guilt was imprinted on you and it remains there even now. You tried to rebel in your own way, but ultimately you failed."

Sarah realizes too late that she should not have chosen that last word with Hadassah, but goes on, "…And one more difference is that my grandmother was always loving towards me. She was a survivor in every sense of the word, and knew how to make things go her way even in the worst of circumstances. I admired that and so I identified with her- not my parents. Unfortunately, you did not have such a savior in your life. My grandmother kept a Kosher home so I asked her if she believed in God. She said she had her doubts after what she had seen in the camp, but she followed the rules — just in case. Again, that survivor instinct!"

I'm lying to her. I actually resented my grandmother — she was the living reminder of all the misery, horror, and tortures that my parents had believed they had divinely eluded. Her mere presence gave off an odor of despondency; she was literally accompanied by a cloud of bitterness, which resulted in severe consequences to my whole family. My parents were unable to escape from it; eventually they surrendered to it altogether, no longer believing in the miraculous. I probably hated her because it was she who chose to implant that caustic kernel that had hardened us all until all the joy of living just went poof! Hadassah so reminds me of her — a wretch of a woman who lived only to infect everyone in sight with her pestilence...just listening to her sickens me...I loathe her — this Holocaust survivor!

With a start, Sarah allows herself to look again at Hadassah. She was more than aware that she had transferred her deeply ingrained repugnance for her grandmother directly onto her patient. She just hoped Hadassah was not aware of it. To redirect the conversation, she turned towards a safer subject by asking:

"Did your parents follow the Torah?"

"Yes, they were super religious, but I became an atheist to further distance myself from them."

Wishing to reach some sort of accord here, Sarah admits,

"I became an atheist as well — we are more alike than you think."

Hadassah's incredulity shows clearly on her face. Her upturned eyebrows and curled sneer spoke volumes, but Sarah forges ahead, wanting to confront this quickly disintegrating relationship head-on before they both became entombed in quicksand:

"I see by your expression that you don't agree with what I just said. That's why I have to ask what you think of me."

Hadassah holds nothing back:

"I am envious of you and resent your success. As you just pointed out, we come from similar backgrounds, but just look at your life compared to mine. Let's be honest here — if you are capable of that."

Then she said the words that all therapists fear: "I don't even feel like living anymore."

Hadassah sits back in her chair, her body relaxed as if she had just thrown aside all of her burdensome memories. She does not look up at Sarah, she does not seek her response, and she appears listless, as if she had finally abandoned whatever it was that was keeping her going from day to day, year after year. Hadassah had set herself adrift on her final journey, but Sarah either did not recognize that fact, or refused to give up on this patient who was so like herself.

Once again, Sarah tries to engage Hadassah, "Are you contemplating killing yourself? If so we really need to talk about it."

Hadassah rises from her chair with more energy than she had ever shown before:

"I'm not confiding in you. I have known you for a while and I do not think I will ever be able to trust or even like you! I had a modicum of faith in Diane, but you are nothing like her."

Refusing to give up, Sarah tries reaching her with a different tactic:

"I believe it is possible for us to establish a relationship, but that takes some time. Can we go back to our earlier conversation about your feelings about losing people? Did you feel any regret or sorrow when your parents died?"

Hadassah replies vehemently,

"Absolutely not! I felt no guilt either - I was actually elated when I heard the news — both times! I felt freed of all the bleakness. As I said before, I was nurtured on a placenta of guilt — my mother passed it onto me in the womb and my father gave me a booster shot of it every year of my life! I don't know if you're familiar with a recent study on the children of Holocaust survivors. No? I'm not surprised — your hackneyed methods expose you as being behind the times. Anyway, it's known as epigenetic inheritance and researchers found that people like me inherit stress and trauma THROUGH THEIR DNA! So, I'm not crazy — it's a scientific fact! I'm not to blame — it's been passed down to me genetically. So why shouldn't I have rejoiced when those two, whose genes malformed my very soul, disappeared forever?"

Hadassah stands defiantly in the middle of the room now. It is clearly evident that she is speaking more to herself than to Sarah, confronting those demons lurking in the corners of her heart.

Still hopeful that she can reach Hadassah, Sarah tries reasoning with her patient:

"That study, while I have not read it, refers to the children of Holocaust survivors, but you have told me that your parents escaped the scourge altogether. Besides, what you are describing sounds very much like Jung's theory of the Collective Unconscious which puts forth the idea that all of us share the same feelings buried deep within our psyches."

Hadassah is infuriated at what she sees as another example of Sarah's feelings of superiority towards her. Sarah feels her annoyance so she continues in a placating tone:

"You may not be aware of your true feelings because you have understandably repressed them in order to survive. However, that life saver only works for so long; it doesn't make them go away forever. When allowed to go unrecognized, repressed feelings continue to influence us unless we become more conscious of them. For example, you claim that you are not angry with Diane for leaving you, but you are! You're just not ready to accept that anger. Most therapists believe that depression is anger turned inward against ourselves. In our first session, you admitted that you have been angry all your life and that strong emotion has made you depressed all your life."

"You're just mixing me up to make more money here. You know nothing about me, which is why I don't believe anything you say."

Then, shaking her head from side to side, much like a child does during a tantrum, Hadassah replies with a rigorous finality,

"No, I don't think you can help me, and I really don't like you, Sarah. You're just too sure of yourself, speaking to me in that high-and-mighty voice."

She nastily mimics Sarah by repeating her words in a snide drone:

"Borderline personality – Repression – Depression…Jung…Collective Unconscious…blah-blah-blah! I could get more out of reading some self-help book online." Hadassah finally delivers her final ultimatum: "I'm quitting therapy."

Sarah is fuming inside, blurting out what sounds like a rebuke to Hadassah:

"M-m-m-m, sounds like what you did at eighteen. You are leaving here without devising a reasonable plan to help yourself. That's what's called being self-destructive in my circle. What's even worse, you would be repeating your past patterns. It's called repetition compulsion and…"

Hadassah now stopped her before she could say another word.

"I'm not at all interested in your diagnosis or your circle-of-friends for that matter. You like showing off your smarts in front of me. I think you just want to humiliate me because it makes you feel superior. You need that feeling to give you a reason to go on. In a nutshell, you think you're better than me."

Sarah knows better than to argue with a patient in that state of mind so she changes her tactics by agreeing or "joining the resistance" rather than trying to shoot it down.

"I guess I will just have to lay back more and not try to change you. I often make that mistake even as a therapist. Maybe I can learn from you."

Sarah's new approach fails miserably; Hadassah appears unaffected by Sarah's submission, instead warning her,

"Well, I may be forced to take a different path and give up fixing myself. I have lost interest in going any further with this."

Sarah also feels drained of any kind of optimism at this point. She has given it her best, but can't seem to make any headway. This was a new sensation for her — losing, so she ends the session with a silly joke:

"Well, I hope you don't do anything foolish when you leave here. Oops…there I go again, meddling like a Jewish mother."

The irony was not lost or appreciated by Hadassah:

"Good one — are you referring to my mother or yours — maybe both? Perhaps I can leave you with a shared feeling of abandonment as my legacy to you… and you can continue down that spiral of guilt when you hear that you lost a patient."

With that, Hadassah slipped out of the office and Sarah's life forever.

Sarah shook away the misgivings she felt after this session – Hadassah was just being overly dramatic. She had dealt with patients like her before. Yet, her own feelings of guilt and inadequacy may have contributed to her not being on her game…had her own regressions contributed to what had just occurred with Hadassah? What about that telltale countertransference from her grandmother to Hadassah? That certainly didn't help either of them! Sarah was afraid to face her own fears — all those years of therapy lost…had she been fooling herself and her patients? She had allowed her own emotions to cloud her skills as a therapist…why had she reacted so furiously when Hadassah mimicked her? Sarah knew the answer; her mother repeated things she said back to her in the same mocking tones that Hadassah had used. The very memory of it made her fly into a whirlwind of wrath — she, trying to explain to her mother why she had to go to the library every night, and her mother imitating her pleas with vicious laughter. Her mother knew the real reason she wanted to go there and Sarah hated her for knowing it. She felt like a filthy whore then — the very title her parents had bestowed upon her so long ago. Even now, Sarah was unable to rid herself of that curse — even now, she wanted to indulge herself in lewd fantasies…shouldn't she have vanquished those unnatural thoughts by now?

But wait - years of analysis had taught her that those thoughts and memories were not lewd, hadn't they? She had grown smug about her accomplishments, lulled into a false sense of security that had multiplied with each successful treatment. Sarah knew it was time for her to return once again to her own therapy sessions if she was to be able to help her patients, especially Hadassah. She looked at her watch and saw it was time to leave. In times like these, Sarah always reverted back and found comfort in her instinctual will to beat any odds at any cost; she knew it was priceless and that it was in her DNA.

She left feeling more optimistic, despite what she had just realized about herself. Sarah opened the door to her office, her mind inundated with the faces of her patients, past and present… Stella…Pauline…George…Catherine…Paul…Barry and Gladys… and especially Hadassah.

Thus, she was totally unprepared for the news that came the next day: Hadassah had placed her father's fully loaded revolver in her mouth and pulled the trigger. She had chosen to die alone in the most violent way she knew…who was there to care about the mess she left behind?

CHAPTER 9

GROUP SESSION – MONTH 7
THE GATHERING

With even more trepidation than she felt then, Sarah stood before the same door she had faced seven months earlier. This time, she again had to counsel her patients as they confronted the reality of death; the exception now was that she could be held responsible for Hadassah's suicide. When Diane had died, she was more of a surrogate at best and a usurper at worst. Now, this same group of men and women (minus the one that has finally gained prominence based solely upon her absence) may well deem Sarah to be the catalyst and even the reason for Hadassah's devastating decision.

Sarah had answered the insistently ringing phone that had jangled her out of her restive sleep…she had forgotten all about Hadassah because she was concentrating more on her own dilemma. Hadassah's accusations were unsettling, to say the least…and Sarah could not face them, so her mind wandered away to seek healing through sleep. As a trained therapist, she knew this signified depression, but instead of fighting the impulse, she succumbed to it, weakened by the strain of Hadassah's attacks and her own self-doubt and disappointment.

The voice on the other end was detached: "Dr. S, I am a neighbor of one of your patients, Hadassah. I found your number in a note she left on the fridge. It explicitly said to call you so that's what I'm doing. Hadassah shot herself last night and she's dead. I didn't really know her — she was just the old woman next door — quiet, not too friendly — which was fine with me...who needs a nosy, needy neighbor — if you know what I mean. Anyway, she's Jewish so the coroner came and took her away real quick. She's going to be buried with her parents somewhere. So that's all I know..." Before Sarah could ask about more details, the phone went silent — dead and cold in her hands. Hadassah had said her final goodbye, appropriately enough, through this unfeeling stranger. She had wanted Sarah to hear and see what her life was like — ignored, isolated, and insignificant. The guilt arrow was expertly aimed and imbedded into Sarah's heart.

Sarah slowly opens the door and stands before this group of faces now so familiar to her. Despite the closeness she had established with them, she anxiously scans their eyes and body language to see if she could detect any hints of hostility or anger towards her. No doubt due to her recent loss of confidence, Sarah hears her voice quiver as she begins:

"I believe that you have already heard the tragic news about Hadassah's suicide, and I want to spend our time here today discussing your feelings and reactions. We need to confront the fact of her suicide now before you have the chance to let it fester and interfere with your own healing process. So at this point, I just want to hear what you felt when you first heard the news and then, how you feel now after you have had time to think it over...Who would like to go first?"

Sarah is hoping that Paul will take the lead, as he had in that very first session. They had made considerable progress in the past seven months so she wanted him to lead the discussion in the right direction. To her dismay and horror, it is Stella who first speaks...Stella, who has made the least progress towards any type of empathy or self-awareness. Thus, Sarah is not at all surprised when Stella begins with a distasteful analysis:

"I honestly don't know why she offed herself like that. What a mess! She was always so absorbed in her own problems…my God, the Holocaust happened in the last century and neither she nor her parents were even there! So many times I wanted to tell her to get over it already. You want to talk about problems? (Here, Stella glared at the rest of the group, jerking her head to face each one of them. Sarah thought Stella was going to spin her head around like that demon-infested Linda Blair in *The Exorcist* if she wasn't careful.) I face a beating every time I return from this group. First, he asks me what we talk about in here, and then he wants to know about what's wrong with each and every one of you. If I say anything, he jumps at me, telling me that I better not be humiliating him with my stories. I get so mad! So I tell him about how you all keep telling me to leave him, that I'm too good for him, and that I should find a safe haven. Then his face gets really red and I feel that first hard whack on my face and then a sharper slap on my ass. I fight back as hard as I can, but as usual, he gets the better of me. Oh, what can I do-o-o-o?"

Fully aware of Stella's intention to turn this session into "The Stella Hour," Sarah tries to bring her back to the topic at hand:

"How did you hear about Hadassah?"

"On the TV of course…that's big news in this two-bit town. I made the mistake of telling my husband that she was in my group. He criticized you, Sarah – he said that you must be a lousy shrink and that I was wasting my time and his money. Of course, I defended you. (Stella looks over at Sarah with that same eerie winking grin that Sarah always finds so unsettling.) We got into a mess of a fight over it — look at my bruises!" (She proudly displays the marks on her arms and thighs, which once again reminds Sarah of the claret red marks she was so honored to see in the mirror after her father had spanked her.)

That little tickle he imparted when he slowly passed his other hand over my buttocks…it was so pleasurable. The red marks brought that sensation back to me over and over again. It was when I first realized that pain could lead to pleasure…Just like my fantasy about Stella's alternating sweetness and cruelty. She knows my secret, as well as her own…her bruises recall that maddening sensuality, much like Proust's Madeleine.

Sarah stirs herself back into the present. Stella is still giving a blow-by-blow (literally) description of last night's fight. The group had heard all of this before; Stella is completely cut off from them… selfishly apathetic to their suffering and grief over Hadassah's death. She is just not ready to deal with her own raw feelings, but the others can't see that side of her.

Finally, overwhelmed by his own emotions, George interrupts Stella's monologue:

"Jeez Stella, what the hell is wrong with you?"

Stella can't believe her ears – George attacking her at a time like this! Of course, they were often at odds with one another due to the fact that he cares too much, and she cares too little. He feels for *everything* and she feels for *nothing*…at least, that's how they appear to each other.

"Forgive me for living here! For God's sake George, how many times have I had to listen to your whining and sobbing about your spoiled and psychotic son??? You are pathetic — and everybody feels the same way about you — don't we?"

Stella peers at the rest of the group, searching for any signs of support, but many of them cannot meet her glance.

"That's right - just keep on letting George go down that same old road — full of detours, but always ending up in the same place!"

Sarah realizes that she is quickly losing control here and knows she has to somehow bring the focus back to Hadassah…but she flounders: *Am I too scared of returning to the subject of Hadassah? Have I completely lost my way on this journey of self-discovery? I have to get back on track and soon!*

Reverting to her knowledge and expertise, Sarah is relieved as she hears herself steering the discussion towards an analysis of what had just transpired between Stella, George and the rest of the group:

"OK, let's see what we can glean from this confrontation…I have spoken to all of you, either in your individual sessions or in the group meetings, about the continuum of feeling. Some of you are at one end of this spectrum — you feel too much and are too concerned about just about everyone. George is at that end of the continuum, and he has lots of company in here. On the other hand, some of you are too unfeeling about others. You are more concerned with what is going on in your life…too self-absorbed to care about other people's problems, and unable to fully participate in mentalization. You all remember that term and what it means, yes?"

The group dutifully nods their heads, with some of them ruefully… and silently acknowledging their failures in that area. While Stella appears embarrassed by the question, Sarah doubts that she truly understands just how far over she is situated on the apathy side.

"We have discussed why it would be better to be somewhere in the middle of that line — sort of like the Goldilocks model — not too soft…not too hard…but just right!" Having injected some humor into what had been a tense atmosphere, Sarah sees the group literally exhale a collective sigh of relief.

Taking the reins once again, Sarah turns to George, asking him what had motivated him to lash out at Stella the way he did.

"I couldn't stomach Stella's attitude any longer. She was just the same old Stella – monopolizing the discussion with her tales of woe, not showing a whit of regret about Hadassah, but actually criticizing the woman after she was dead. I felt I had to defend her because she was not here to do it for herself. I was also really shaken up by Hadassah's suicide…it was truly devastating to see how someone sitting here in the midst of all of us could hide her despair so well. Sure, she looked sad, but never suicidal-at least not to me. I was over-whelmed just thinking about how I missed the signs. Was I too dis-missive, too ignorant, or just too apathetic towards her? I felt that I had not only betrayed Hadassah, but myself as well. Maybe I am not the caring person I think I am…maybe I'm just being too self-ish here, worrying more about my own problems — kind of like Stella…" He looks to Sarah for some sort of comfort.

He is vocalizing what I am thinking about myself, my profession, my whole life. The difference is that I am not even asking the questions – I already know the answers to them all too well.

Sarah smiles gently at George. "No one would ever accuse you of apathy or selfishness, dear George…in fact, you are the most caring person in the room right now. How about the rest of you — how do you feel about Hadassah's killing herself?"

Barry looks uncomfortable, but feels he has to say something. He had good manners — the kind who automatically asked oth-ers, "How are you?" without actually listening to their answers.   In that way, Barry could be labeled superficial, but Sarah knew his mannerisms were actually his method of self-preservation. Barry was afraid of confrontation — even with his own emotions — and so he tended to minimize events:

"Well, of course it was an awful thing to hear — especially about someone I knew — but what can you do? She was unhappy all of her life…we knew that from what she said in here…a few therapy sessions won't cure a lifetime of misery, will they? So, I don't feel guilty about it and I don't think you should either, George!"

Barry said the name George, but was he actually addressing me? Did he sense my own feelings of guilt? Had he become adept at mentalization? Well, at least I accomplished something in here…

But then Catherine interrupts Sarah's train of thought:

"Wait just a minute here…there is certainly someone in this room who should take the blame – SARAH!"

All eyes turn towards their therapist to see her reaction, but Catherine will not yield just yet:

"Yes, she is the trained psychotherapist here-not you, George, not you Barry, not you Stella, and certainly not me!"

Catherine's obsessive desire for control is in full gear now; she yearns to take over the group discussion, just as she wants to take over everyone's destiny — her family's, her daughter-in-law's, Sarah's, the other members of the group — and ultimately her own. Blaming others was Catherine's game plan for survival and now she was eager to place the blame squarely on Sarah for not doing more to help Hadassah.

"What kind of therapist are you Sarah? Couldn't you see that Hadassah was giving up on herself AND YOU? But you just abandoned her — your incompetence is stupefying!"

Of course she's right. I let my own feelings of self-doubt cloud my judgement - I was selfish, much more than George believed himself to be-because I should have known better! Catherine's accusations are right on the money. I should be stripped of my license to practice…and publicly punished for my sins.

Sarah is on the verge of breaking down. The guilt she had been feeling since first hearing about Hadassah was now hell-bent on destroying her. Catherine's onslaught of insults crashes around her, each one a severe blow to Sarah's self-image, and they were now hitting their targets with pitiless precision. Suddenly Paul's voice could be heard above the fray. It is a quiet interjection, yet spoken authoritatively enough for a cease-fire.

"We have to stop playing the Blame Game in this sacred place. We should all be above that by now. Yes, I am deeply saddened by Hadassah's death, just like everyone in this room including Sarah. It's only natural to be upset by what happened, but we must understand both as individuals and as a group that what Hadassah did should not be blamed on any of us. Nor should we allow it to halt our own journeys towards self-discovery and healing. We are all pilgrims in here. (Paul intentionally focuses on Sarah, fully aware of her internal conflict and self-recriminations.) We began as one group traveling together; we have told our tales; we have cried, laughed, and screamed at one another. Now one of us has made the decision not to go on, but we must not allow her choice to prevent us from completing our pilgrimage. We walk at different paces, but we walk as one — shoring one another up when necessary and building bridges as we go."

Paul's eyes are brimming with tears, a rare show of emotion so powerful that it stops Catherine's rants at once. Sarah always knew that Paul would be her knight, noble and courageous, and a worthy companion to her. He had picked up the torch and passed it over to Sarah, just as she believed he would. Now Sarah knew she could continue working with this group, while working on herself at the same time. The race was not over; her energy was not depleted. The journey would continue… and so she faced the group once more.

"Paul, thank you for reminding us about why we are here in this room together. Pauline, we need to hear from you now."

Pauline stands up uneasily. Sarah could see she was anxious.

"I am more worried than ever. First Diane and now Hadassah… Death is such a certainty; no ifs, ands, or buts about it. I never really thought about the finality of death before, but now that I am about to become a mother, I have to admit that these recent deaths have had a serious impact on me. What if I die early…what will happen to my child? What about my child dying before me? I think I have made a huge mistake — my life was so simple before…now I have added a deep wrinkle to it, one that is so much more than skin-deep. What was I thinking?"

Pauline's fears mirrored my own misgivings about having children. My mother died early — from cancer when she was fairly young. Did she pass that gene onto me — in the same way that Hadassah had inherited her mother's depression while she was still in the womb? Worse yet, would I pass that poison pill onto my own children? I go to the doctor religiously for prescribed check-ups and pester my own children (even my surrogate child) to do the same. Pauline and I are battling the same hellion; I have to help her if I am to help myself.

"Pauline, remember that Hadassah made the choice to die, something that I am certain you would never even contemplate. As for Diane, well many of you are not aware that Diane was fighting depression while she was leading this group. While it is not a proven fact, many experts feel that depression may indirectly lead to an early death. Depression is so overpowering that it saps your energy, making you less likely to take steps to remain healthy, such as exercising, eating the right foods, or even going to doctors on a regular basis. Once again Pauline, I do not think you fall into that category. The extraordinary steps you are taking to have a child of your own confirm your optimistic outlook on life. Bringing children into this world, whether on your own or through another person, is the most hopeful choice someone can make because it signifies that you believe in the future."

Sarah then speaks directly to the entire group:

"So you see that we all have different reactions to Hadassah's death: anger, fear, anxiety, sadness…none of these feelings are wrong. What is important here is that we all feel some emotion. We are all capable of feeling anything; if it makes you feel good about yourself, hold onto it, but if it makes you feel horrible, allow it to pass away. I have encouraged all of you not to obsess about the destructive events that happened in your past or about the loss of loved ones who may or may not have hurt you in some way. Instead dwell upon your good memories. Speak positively about them: what they gave to you and what you learned from them. Discuss how they helped you grow as a person so that the group can recognize a similarity and learn from your own awareness."

Sarah then redirects the discussion back to Hadassah.

"In the same way, you should benefit from what happened to Hadassah, no matter how difficult that may be. We all must try to move on after a given period of time. Everyone should follow his or her own timetable though, and be aware that Hadassah is not suffering now, even though we still grieve for her and ourselves. We have learned over the past seven months that it does no good to cling to memories that sadden or upset us. Break away from that roadway of negativity by reflecting on the positive events in your lives. I am here to help you find your own way just as I am relying on you to accompany me on this journey. You are not alone… please be assured of that."

As if awakening from a deep sleep, the group stretches out their arms and stand together as one. Sarah feels assured that they have finally cohered as a group. They depart, linked together in their resolve to persevere on their voyage. The door closed behind them, but Sarah knew it would remain open for the remainder of their time together.

My mind is going a mile a minute, yet I feel strangely at peace, as if I was half-way through a marathon. Images swirl around me…my father and mother, flawed yes, but loving parents nonetheless. The sharp pangs of blame and condemnation that usually accompanied their ghosts have dissipated somewhat. My mother's greatest pains were suffered in silence and my father's guilt over his perceived sins wrought havoc on his own self-worth. Much of what happened between them and me was no one's fault. It has taken this group of seven penitents to teach me how to use my tainted visions not to attempt to shore up a crumbling foundation, but instead to demolish the vulnerable structure I had erected and start anew.

CHAPTER 10

SARAH THE LOST PILGRIM

Sarah had started to masturbate again, usually in the early morning to jumpstart her day…and then again in the late evening, just before going to bed, to calm herself to sleep. Lately, that was the only way she could even approach the energy level she needed to face what was to come, or, once the day was done, to lower the anxiety that was now tearing her insides apart. While the morning and evening sessions seemed to contradict each other in purpose, Sarah knew just how to manipulate her strokes to achieve what she wanted. Even the orgasms differed: in the morning, she reached one quickly, leaving her body aching for another one. That longing kept her going until the later one, which was administered skillfully and slowly, often accompanied by her favored dildo inserted smoothly into her anus, until her orgasms came one after the other in a rising crescendo of whispered sighs and high-pitched squeals. Afterwards, spent and exhausted, she would tumble down deeply into her welcoming mattress, ready to indulge herself with erotic dreams bordering on rapture.

PAUL:
Sarah's sessions with Paul were going well. They had made considerable progress together, so much so that their trust in one another

was absolute. Paul revealed his hidden desires and fantasies to Sarah without holding back: his attraction towards a transgender as well as his erotic dalliances with him; his strong arousal towards his male partner when he dressed in women's clothing; his early sexual experimentation with girls…the more Paul spoke, the more Sarah wanted him, not just as a friend, but as a lover too. Paul seemed to be teasing her into believing that such a relationship was possible, but Sarah feared she was allowing her desires and her imagination dictate her course of action here. Paul's first proclamation could not be denied…as a result of their work together, he was secure in pursuing the life of a gay man — something he had sought since childhood. How could Sarah deny Paul this breakthrough that they had so diligently vied to achieve? While she had her doubts that this was the only path open for him, she worried that her physical attraction for him was motivating her therapeutic guidelines, something that she NEVER had given way to before. Professional ethics had always been her guidepost. Above all, she did not want to lose Paul as a patient so she held back, at least on the surface.

Paul reminds me of myself in so many ways. In college, I identified with the male students. I majored in math since that was traditionally a "male" subject at the time. As one of only two females in those classes, I bonded with the men. I wore pants and flirted with the co-eds, just to test my sexuality. I felt freer there — allowing myself to experiment with the social mores of the time. While it's true, there were consequences (being black-balled by a teacher from Phi Beta Kappa for my masculine leanings), I regret none of it. Yes, I engaged in sex with women — in fact, one of those relationships bordered on love, but I was never a full-fledged lesbian…I just had to know that the choice was mine to make, not one dictated by society or my parents or my peers. I prided myself on being a true rebel…but was my stance real or just a way for me to stand out from the crowd?

That is why I still believe in my heart that Paul cannot be gay — he breathes sexuality whenever we are together. He seemed open to my idea to mix things up a bit, having sex with a man and a woman at the same time to "test the waters" and see which one he really prefers. He's already told me how he was turned on by men who dressed as women — then why not try the real thing for once? Have a real woman wear a strap-on first to make him more comfortable…she could take him as any man, but then he could have a go at it…At least, that is what I secretly desire for him and me – I feel I found my soulmate, but I may just be kidding myself into believing him to be "the one" because I am so lost and alone.

At the end of their most recent session, Sarah had cautiously advanced the concept of a ménage a trois to him just to gauge his reaction. Paul's face told her that her idea was not altogether foreign to him and yet, he seemed distraught. Had she unknowingly evoked a shameful memory in him? Or had he been having the same salacious thoughts about her? That night, Sarah blissfully remembered the last fantasy she had that day during Paul's session — only now it came back to her in a dream:

Paul reached for me after I finished my suggestion…he had a strap-on dildo in his grasp and held it before me invitingly. Without speaking, he stripped me from the waist down, leaving only my bra and loosened blouse to cover my breasts. Then he fitted the strap-on over my vagina with a deliberate scrutiny. As he quickly undressed, I saw that he had an obvious erection. I climbed aboard him, watching his smooth buttocks gracefully react to my touch…as I plunged myself into him, his body vibrated…it seemed to be humming. We moved together as one for a while and then he came all at once — his frenzied orgasm was so strong. He rested for a moment and then arose from the floor with a single purpose — to take me.

I obligingly turned over so that he could enter me anally – I imagined that he preferred it that way, but to my surprise, he flipped me over, removing the strap-on in one swift move. He licked his fingers and then roughly inserted them into my vagina — two at a time. Foreplay was unnecessary — our recent encounter had more than readied me. He forced my legs apart and then he was inside of me. My vagina had hungered for him for so long that she hugged him tightly, unwilling to let go. My orgasm was upon me before I knew it, but Paul did not stop there. He was a generous lover, granting me multiple orgasms before reversing my prone position so that he could now do what came naturally to him. I didn't mind — we succumbed together one last time before separating our bodies.

Sarah giggled in her sleep. Of course, none of this was real, but the fantasy was pure enough to suffice for now.

The next morning, Sarah went back to masturbating so that she could feel alive again. Although the last group session (post-Hadassah's suicide) had ended well, Sarah was still having difficulty finding her center. She was punishing herself with solitary confinement; masturbation, by nature, was a lonely activity and Sarah realized she was taking a risk following such a daily and nightly regimen. This was not the right time for such isolation, not in the midst of her desolate conflict; Sarah was all too aware of what she was undertaking — surrendering to her darker nature, yet she would not…or could not stop it.

I am surrounded by images of death – Diane, Maria – even my grandmother and parents — each of them haunting me with these disturbing flashbacks. I hear my grandmother's voice echoing my mother's hissing — "Sarah, you may as well be a common prostitute — the way you behave. That boy with the leering look, always sniffing around our door — and you scurrying to meet him on some corner, like a wind-blown leaf all tattered to shreds by its fate!" Were they trying to save me in the only way they knew how — with insults and degradation? Yes, it was true - I bolted to him, even though I had learned what he was about the hard way…but he was my simplest and most direct escape route, sort of like those fire drills we went through at school. My home was ablaze with abuse, physical and emotional, and my instinct was to race out of the inferno. How was I to know that I was actually jumping out of the proverbial frying pan into the fire? Well, they're equally unbearable, except that one was quicker. Better to die on-the-run — in an instant — before you have time to change your mind…

I understood Maria and Hadassah better now — both opted for lightning-quick relief from their tormented souls — maybe they would find peace in the afterlife. But what about Diane and my mother? Why did they choose a slower death? Both of them willed themselves to die… proven beyond any doubt by my mother's agonizing wait for her sure-to-return breast cancer and Diane's laissez-faire attitude towards the well-known symptoms of her heart disease. Just like Maria and Hadassah, they were too overwhelmingly weakened by depression and so they chose to self-destruct in a more subtle way. No, they did not jump into a river or pull the trigger, but their choice to not address or even try to change what they believed to be their fate was nonetheless suicidal.

During the last year of her life, my mother would endlessly lament the loss of her past loved ones: "Sarah, everyone I knew is now gone from this earth…I feel so alone. I think about your father every day and pray that I will leave before he does." She felt no joy, certainly not in me, no — not even in her grandchildren. Only now can I empathize with her fear and despair. Many of my friends are no longer alive at this point…even my first husband — the man who loved me in the freshness of my youth — is gone. How strange that I should mourn that loss, but we had been giddily happy in those early years… He could not keep his hands off of me back then… they were not delivering the punches that later tore us apart. No, I thrilled when he looked at me with such longing — no one had ever yearned for me like that. Our lovemaking was endless, staying in bed for days on end, just to embrace the exhilaration of our newly minted passion. His arms encircled me in a protective way. I felt so safe with him. So, his death saddened me; I was surprised by the depth of my regret…but I believe my distress was caused by the fact that the one person whose memories of me were that of a girlish bride was no longer around to keep those images alive.

As to my mother's lingering melancholy, at the time I only blanketed myself with that same old resentment towards her, which made me not only unsympathetic, but also apathetic to her misery. I should have urged her to remember the past with hope, not despair — as I have done countless times to save my patients who were in a similar downward spiral. Yet, I could not bring myself close enough to want to help her. As for Diane, she never confided in me and so I let her drift away from me, helplessly — but my

God… I could have saved them! Aren't I known as "The Fixer?" Or is that just another masquerade?

Sarah places her hands over her ears, trying to deafen the voices she hears…but since they are speaking from within her, the gesture is a futile one. To quiet them, she decides to indulge herself in what had become an unbreakable habit. As she bends over the ornately designed chilly metal footboard of her bed (*the same bed where my second marriage began and ended — why have I kept it with me all these years?*), prepared to begin her early morning routine, she absentmindedly positions a large makeup mirror so she can clearly watch her hands and fingers as they stroke her backside. She was taught to use such a mirror by her first sex therapist to heighten her delight as she masturbated. Into her early thirties, Sarah had had difficulty reaching orgasm so she would fake them just as so many women do. In her case, she was not only sexually inhibited by her early experiences (the abusive uncle, the spankings given by her father, the rape by her first boyfriend, the resulting abortion), but she lacked the ability to yield to anyone or anything. So her therapist had her hold up a mirror to watch herself completely and thus happily lose the inhibitions that had been freezing her insides.

Thus, her morning masturbation always included that familiar tool. She watched her hand movements gentle at first, then morphing into pats and quickening slaps, which bring a familiar claret-like blush to her rear cheeks – *I've seen that shade of red before — so satisfying and just as stimulating now as it was then* — pushing Sarah to start her manipulations in earnest. Sarah always hesitates before reaching that final climax — she wants to hold on to that unbelievable blend of ecstasy and anticipation for a moment longer — and then all at once, she yields to it, staring at her face and body in the mirror as they crumple into sheer joy. Afterwards, she pulls away from the brass footboard and is startled by an unwelcome vision. Sarah flings the mirror away from her, but it stubbornly comes to rest by the pillows, completely upright so that its reflection may be clearly seen by one and all.

I see a shadowy figure in that looking-glass, but whose? Hadassah's face floats near mine, scarred and as bloody as Banquo's ghost appeared to Macbeth. She does not look at peace, but more as she did at our final session together. I am claret-red all over now, ashamed that she was a jealous witness to my pleasure. I know I should engage her, but am just as discomfited by her presence now as I was before. She grimaces at me with that same haggard look, made even grimmer after the harsh reality of her suicide. Once again, I am reminded of my failure as a therapist, as a friend, and as a daughter. I look at the mirror again and the image slowly retreats back into the hell-hole from which it came. I am depleted, but something is driving me forward…oh yes, Stella.

STELLA

Sarah's frustration level is increasing every time she meets with Stella. While it is true that their sessions have become far less confrontational than they were in the beginning, Stella's progress has lagged far behind that of the rest of the group (with, of course, the notable exception being Hadassah). While her earlier diagnosis of Stella displaying borderline symptoms had clarified Sarah's perceptions and treatment plan, she found herself constantly being waylaid by Stella's probing influence. Whenever Sarah would attempt to direct her focus on Stella's therapeutic needs as a borderline patient, Stella would simply sidle away in the wink of her eye.   Just as with Hadassah, she is sickened by Stella's resistance to change, which Sarah views as a contagious pestilence. Acid scourges her throat and it is almost impossible to conceal her disgust as Stella reviews the revolting details of her marital relationship ad nauseam.

Could it be possible that Stella thinks that by consistently taking on the role of victim she is making progress? Or could it be that she savors describing all of the gory, disturbing imagery of her physical encounters — the beatings, the forced sodomies, the humiliations he imposes upon her, the pathetic apologies and false promises made over and over again? How can I get through to her so that she stops this cycle before it kills her? Have I somehow made her believe that these revelations would bring us closer? Have I subconsciously revealed too much of myself to her?

As if hearing her thoughts, Stella impulsively takes Sarah in her arms.

"I know you feel my agonies...you've been there, caught in that same web of lust and gratification. I am no longer ashamed of what is happening to me, because I am aware that nothing can happen to me except what I secretly desire to happen. You've helped me understand how I am not really a masochist, but just the opposite. He is fooled into thinking he controls me — body and soul — but in reality, I am the one in charge. I laugh inwardly as he crawls to me, sniveling like the child that he is, begging for my forgiveness and my pity. I am addicted to that feeling, which is why I will tolerate whatever he does to me just so that afterwards, I hold the power in my hands! Oh Sarah, you know that feeling – I feel it whenever I look into your eyes — power is the ultimate aphrodisiac."

I have created a monster. I thought I was in the business of healing people, remaking them into the best they could possibly be, but Stella is not whole; she is half-baked, her insides seeping with raw emotions that threaten to spill over, sweeping away whatever is in its way at any time. Her naked vulnerability attracts me though...I long to castigate her soft flesh into submission until I own her, until she stops wanting to be on top and simply gives into me mindlessly. Then she would be free...then I would be a true mender. Finally, I would be comfortable letting her go....but how to overpower and empower both of us at the same time?

Sarah's ears pick up Stella's rant; she is now venting about George's treatment of her at the last group session. Sarah could see that she was hurt and bent on revenge — not a great outcome for any of her patients, but especially not for Stella who feels entitled to express her thoughts with abandon, and George, who would acutely feel each and every barb until he would finally retreat from her assaults. At that point, Sarah would have to start again, rebuilding his fractured self-image after having nearly glued him back together.

"Wait until I see that old broken-down excuse for a man next time! He won't dare open his yap to me or anyone else, I can promise you that. Just because he's an unhappy and miserable soul doesn't mean he has the right to take me down with him. All the others were on my side – Sexy Paul, Bitchy Catherine, Smug Barry, and even Goody-Goody Pauline – you could see that, couldn't you?"

Sarah has to stifle the guffaw about to explode out of her mouth — those nicknames were definitely amusing — but then Stella's eyes narrow in on Sarah threateningly…Sarah instinctively looks away, unable to meet the gaze of those deeply probing pupils. Now here was her chance to salvage some of the progress she had made with her patients, more for her own sake at this juncture. She carefully measures her words and her tone, trying to find that essential balance between her outward professional authority and her inward vicarious relationship with this particularly troubling patient.

"Each of you brings a unique personality to the group and it is not at all necessary for you to meld together as one unit, or even to agree with one another. However, belonging to such a group necessitates a willingness to both listen and respect the other group members as well as to relinquish self-absorption while the session is in progress."

Stella is willing to take this as a rebuke of George's outburst and so she greets Sarah's analysis with a wide grin. She strokes and then grasps Sarah's arms in a steely, yet seductive way, as only she could.

Her touch is maddening — she wants to exert her power over me by taking advantage of my weakness for her – I have to somehow extricate myself from this whole situation before I lose everything I have worked so hard to achieve…the combination of her and Paul is like a one-two knock-out pummeling. I have that same nagging conviction that I deserve being punished, aching for both of them to chastise me for my thoughts and deeds: the obscene fantasies, the non-stop masturbations, the threesomes, the sodomies, the physical abuses, the rape, the abortions — all swirling together in the filthy whirlpool of past and present sins. Now I turn towards Stella as my dominatrix, forcing me to submit to her subjugations, instructing me to beg for more as she flagellates my body. Paul does not rescue me, but instead becomes the master of us both. I reel away, trying to break free from the imaginary shackles…but my cries and exertions are fruitless.

Abruptly, Sarah stands up, removing Stella's grip from her arm. She must leave the room before Stella goes any further.

"I apologize, but I am not feeling well enough to continue today's session. I must have taken too much sun yesterday or perhaps I am suffering from dehydration. In any case, I do not want my illness to disrupt your session so let's make an appointment for later in the week."

Sarah hears the flimsiness of her excuse; she knows Stella does too by the sly wink she gives her as she responds to her:

"Sure Sarah, whatever you need – I'm always here to give it to you."

And with that, Stella sashays out of the session with a definite bounce in her step. She had almost conquered Sarah this time, but Sarah's new awareness of her own fragile psyche would serve her well the next time they met. For now, she would have to be thankful for this minor victory.

PAULINE

Pauline is solicitous towards Sarah from the very start of their first individual session after the last group meeting. In fact, Pauline had pushed her appointment up, just to be there for Sarah as soon as possible, not realizing that Paul and Stella's sessions had been booked earlier.

"How are you doing? I felt so badly for you in group — hearing about Hadassah's suicide must have been hard enough for you to bear without them ganging up against you!"

Pauline's pity brings welcome relief to Sarah…a comforting cocoon as opposed to the stinging atmosphere that surrounded her with Stella. Her next words bring further redemption:

"We've started on the surrogacy proceedings. I can't tell you how you have helped me overcome my fears over the past few months. I am a changed woman!"

Pauline laughs at this last statement; it has been a running joke between them ever since Sarah retold her favorite light-bulb quip to her during one of their early sessions. Sarah's response echoes Pauline's elation:

"You cannot know how much your decision means to me…you are giving me back my faith in my abilities. I have been quite despondent for a while now, but seeing how you have made a 180 degree turn has lifted me up in a big way."

Fearing that she has revealed too much, Sarah quickly changes the topic to the more practical details, a method that has always succeeded with Pauline.

"So, tell me more about where you are at in the process."

Hearing Sarah's difficulties surprises Pauline, but realizing that her therapist did not want to reveal more, she turns to the question just asked:

"We have placed an ad in the **Boston Globe** as well as the **Chicago Sun-Times** because we want to reach as many people as possible. I am hoping to find a surrogate with my coloration, but of course, having spoken with you about your experience, that qualification is no longer my top priority. I just want a mother who will be able to give her baby over to us without any regrets."

Sarah realizes that she had not updated Pauline enough:

"Well, thirty years ago, finding a surrogate by yourself may have been safe, but now with all the legal difficulties, it's better to find a legitimate, reliable agency to help you get the right surrogate. Nowadays, often people use a gestational surrogate which means using a third party egg and your husband's sperm in the surrogate who now bears the child. That helps with eliminating the genetic tie by the birth mother to the child."

"Oh, I get it. But we still want a mental health evaluation of the surrogate we find. It's one of our requirements before making a final decision. I can think of no one better suited to conduct those tests but you, Sarah. Would you be able to help me with this?"

Sarah hesitates…by refusing, she would be acknowledging her current deficiencies, but is she up to the task right now?

Pauline trusts me so completely — she is the one shining light in the quagmire that has been suffocating me these past months — but do I still have what it takes to know how to judge and advise? Sure, my second husband had started a group for surrogate parents that would serve as a sounding board as well as a guideline to steer them through the bumps in the road, but that was so long ago…

She looks at Pauline's anxious face and sees there what she already knows: her expertise would be vital to this patient, her emotional doppelgänger, at least where motherhood was concerned… how could she refuse her, but more importantly, why?

"I would be honored to conduct those evaluations when the time comes, which I hope will be soon. I can feel your impatience and your excited anticipation. Once the mind is made up, things must move forward. I know that feeling."

"I am so relieved…I thought you would say it would be a conflict of interest."

"No, because by that time, you will no longer be my patient. I have treated you and you have overcome your concerns."

Seeing Pauline's obvious disappointment at hearing the finality of her words, Sarah adds a reassurance:

"Of course, after the baby is yours, you may reach out to me with any questions or share any of your thoughts with me. I will always be there to offer my opinions — you know what a meddler I am!"

"Ok then. I will be in touch with you once we find the surrogate."

Reaching out and enveloping Sarah in a warmly given bear hug (light years away from Stella's hold that bordered on strangulation), Pauline's last words to Sarah are:

"Thank you, my dear friend and guide. I will never forget how you changed my life…"

Pauline reluctantly leaves as Sarah stands to silently watch her walk away. Mixed emotions seethe up…

Possibly, there goes my final success story…her words make my heart soar and sink in tandem. Take heart Sarah – when cold reality paralyzes your steps, turn your mind towards Pauline and venture forth again.

BARRY AND GLADYS – THE FINAL ACT

The couple enters the session, hands clasped together with their eyes on one another. Their dress is more casual now, not as consciously planned as in prior visits. Sarah has a fleeting thought as she gazes at them…*Did they just have sex? They have that conspicuous afterglow that floats in the air and over their bodies. I can just about detect that scent of orgasm.*

Barry sits in the chair and pulls Gladys onto his lap. Her mouth opens, showing her pink tongue, which she tantalizingly wiggles at him. Realizing where they are and that they are not alone, they move apart as Gladys straightens and pulls down her skirt. Sarah waits for them to finish and addresses them in a lightly teasing tone:

SARAH: I must say you both seem to have made considerable headway in just the past month alone. Can you tell me what's been going on — have you progressed into something beyond what we earlier spoke about trying — in other words, have your sexual fantasies become physical realities?

BARRY (speaking first — a definite change): Well Sarah, you could definitely be sure of that. We watched some porn movies for a while.

GLADYS (interrupting him, but laughing at the same time): At first, we were so embarrassed even ordering them online! Their titles were just hilarious — "Spankings and Subjugation" — "The Erogenous Zones of Pauline "...that one really got us — we bought it just for the title — it made us think of our fellow group member!

BARRY: What about "Fanny's Fantasies and Flagellations" or "Daddy's Little Lolita?" They were fun at first, but then they became a bit tedious. We tried to select films we thought would mirror our hidden desires, but they never came close so... (He gives Gladys a wicked smile) we took matters into our own hands.

SARAH: Meaning...?

GLADYS: We went to the next level. First we role-played with me as an innocent harem girl and Barry as the lustful Sultan. At first, we were timid, but then Barry literally grew into the part once I added a few accoutrements, like costumes and props. I discovered an outfit in a Halloween store, complete with flowing silk pants and veils — it looked like the one from that show that's always in reruns...you know the one — with Larry Hagman as an astronaut with a genie in a bottle...I think it was called: "I Dream of Jeanie, or something like that — well, anyway — it did the trick along with a tiny pink switch made of silk and feathers. Barry saw me in that get-up and he took over.

BARRY: What about the dildo I bought?

GLADYS: That came later on. Our first fantasy was played out, with me as your sex slave surrounded by hot pink and red swaths of silk and you lightly whipping me and making love to me for hours...

BARRY: Then she fulfilled my fantasy — no, we did not have another woman join in – Gladys was more than enough for me. (Gladys bends over to kiss him.) She bought a new outfit — black leather boots, complete with a matching corset. I adored the way she spanked me as she called me her "bad boy!" She has an amazing tongue too – I never realized it before. She likes to experiment with it, seeing how far it can reach into all of the openings of my body. I feel completely at her mercy, but I like it and that's something I never thought I would accept.

GLADYS: Barry introduced the dildo for my pleasure, but I almost fainted when he first used it, deftly twisting it further and further into my rear before I could stop him. I tried to push his hand away, but he held both my hands together so tightly that I could not move an inch.

SARAH (in a warning voice): Have you chosen a word to use when either one of you is going too far? I always recommend that device for all relationships that include some sadomasochistic behaviors. Something like "Butterfly," for example, to put on the brakes in place of the word "Stop" since that is commonly used during the sex, and so may easily be misconstrued.

Barry and Gladys reacted with apparent shock at Sarah's suggestion:

GLADYS: But, Sarah, now I like it – I was just taken aback by this new sensation – I had never experienced anything even close to sodomy before.

BARRY: I would never hurt my wife in that way – I knew she would come to enjoy it in time.

Gladys looks searchingly at Barry as a slow realization comes over her.

GLADYS: What do you mean by that? Do you think I'm just a sex toy, willing to do whatever you want — any time you want it? My life does not revolve around you, my dear. I have other responsibilities…like running the house and raising the kids. Sure, the sex is good, but it's not the most important thing in a marriage, is it Sarah?

Before Sarah could reply…

BARRY: Gladys, I'm not going to allow you to take over in here again. You claim you want me to take charge in the bedroom, to stop being a wimp and blaming you for my failures. Well, thanks to Sarah's suggestions, I am now confident in my manhood.

GLADYS: I thought marriage was a two-way street — equal partners and all that — we took a vow to support one another, not one bullying the other!

BARRY: Not when it comes to sex. You made that point abundantly clear, not only in here when you first exposed your sexual desires, but also at home, where you are more than willing to submit to my physical commands. I also believe with all of my heart that our new experiences carry us over outside of the bedroom. We both trust each other more now because we have elected to reveal our vulnerabilities to each other. What's more, I for one feel more respected by you and my children and as a result, much of my anger and frustration has melted away as well as my overeating. Sure, we still argue — it would be weird if we agreed on everything — but those disagreements lack the viciousness of the past. We don't exchange insults now, just issues. And we try to find common ground all the time.

Gladys looked at her husband in chagrin. Of course, he was right — they were much happier now.

GLADYS: I'm sorry. I just want to be sure that you still respect me, that I'm not just some bimbo you want for just one thing.

BARRY: Gladys, you — a bimbo? Nothing could ever be further from my mind. I desire you because I respect you. I think most men feel that way about their wives and lovers. The thrill is being able to satisfy the one person whose admiration is the key to their existence. I want to please you because it pleases me to do so.

Gladys is teary-eyed now. Barry stands tall, leading her out the door. He turns to Sarah:

BARRY: We are making good progress, Sarah – you are right in your assessment. I will call you to make our next appointment. I have to take my wife home now…she needs some bed rest.

He winks at Sarah and they leave.

I was right about Barry's skill at mentalization. He put himself in his wife's place, saw that she was hurting, and told her what she wanted to hear. Their sexual satisfaction is evident, but it was primarily brought about by Barry's new-found ability, not by the wish-fulfillments — those are only secondary. He said that he knew she would like sodomy — it was intuitive — she never brought it up in her revelations - that is mentalization.

I first submitted to sodomy at a fairly young age. I had already been raped once so I wanted my next sexual experience to be of my own choosing.

No longer a virgin, I offered my still-untouched anus to my next lover. You see, I wanted to exert control this time, selecting who, when, where, and most importantly how. It was a brief affair — he was an English professor at a nearby campus who fancied himself as the next James Joyce. I suppose that is why he entered me anally with no hesitation whatsoever. He had a lubricant in the drawer next to his bed — suspiciously handy so I surmised that I was not his first virgin anus. Like Gladys, I tried to stop it once he had started, but he was not having any of that. He was much stronger than me; he pinned my arms beneath my body, raised my rear end on a stained suede pillow nearby, and pumped me until I ached. Afterwards, he brought me to orgasm with his fingers, and to my surprise, I did not have to fake it. I came back for more, climbing the spiral stairway to his hidden lodgings, and submitted to his passion more easily; the more I was sodomized, the more I wanted it. That is probably why he ended our liaison so abruptly. Once he realized that I no longer wanted to resist him, he left me to chase another virgin co-ed. Afterwards, I read some of Joyce's private letters and realized his lecherous behavior was not so original after all. Once again, I was raped even though I believed I had commandeered the entire situation. Of course, Gladys is not me, but just for a moment, I lay helpless on the bed next to her.

CATHERINE

Sarah watches as Catherine stealthily creeped into the room; she is unaware of Sarah's presence and so she flinches when Sarah walks towards her.

"Sarah, I didn't see you there. You gave me quite a fright. My heart is still jumpy..."

Typical of Catherine to push blame onto someone else — never admitting a mistake, never giving in, and never giving up her strong sense of control. Holding back her thoughts, Sarah simply apologizes, but not too sincerely. *Now it is her turn to make amends for her indictment of me during the last group session. Let's see if she is up to the task.*

True to form, Catherine begins with a complaint about a recent conflict with her daughter-in-law concerning the grandchildren:

"I went over there the other day to bring them a special treat — my home-baked lemon meringue pie…my son's favorite dessert when he was a child. When I opened the door with my key, my daughter-in-law practically pounced on me, accusing me of spying on her. Sarah, I know you said she had a borderline personality and that I have to stop trying to change her, but for pity's sake, how I am supposed to react when she attacks me like that? I'm not a punching bag for her to strike at whenever she feels like it. I was just trying to do something nice for my family, including her, but she never sees me in a positive way. I give up!"

She had raised her hands above her head during her tirade, but then lowered them in a slump by her side.

What a drama queen — so much like my mother — always performing the grand gesture…but I cannot allow myself to get distracted again.

"Catherine, why do you enter her house without knocking? How would you feel if she did that to you? Try to put yourself in her place so you won't be so prone to assigning blame. Remember what we have been discussing? You are only asking for trouble if you persist in this conquest over your daughter-in-law. I know you want to give your son and his family what you believe they need, but imposing your will on them will never work. It is you who must change in this family dynamic; stop entering their house without knocking first — and I mean that both literally and figuratively! Once inside, earn their trust by not criticizing what you see or voicing your opinions on what should be done. Even an innocuous dessert can have a hidden meaning to someone like your daughter-in-law."

"What can you possibly mean by saying that to me?"

"Well, does your daughter-in-law bake?"

Catherine practically snorts at this,

"Her? She doesn't even know how to heat up frozen waffles! My son does most of the cooking and cleaning up…she always has one of her famous migraines."

"Can't you see that by bringing over a dessert you made yourself could be seen as a slap in the face by your daughter-in-law? She sees you practically breaking and entering, which is an assault on her privacy to begin with, but then you come bearing a trophy to lord over her. That behavior will not change hers; it will only turn her against you even more."

"So, you think I should just ignore the situation the way you did with Hadassah? That didn't end up being a smart move, did it?"

Blame – Guilt – Shame. Am I ever going to escape this trinity of condemnation? The only answer is the one staring me in the face - help yourself before you can help others.

"We are not talking about me here - only you. I know you think you have the answers for your family, but you don't. Think with your head — stop reacting emotionally. Otherwise, you will end up back at square one, with no "Get out of Jail Free" card. Do you truly want to help them?"

Catherine's jaw juts out at Sarah and her mouth is trembling.

"Of course I do. Why do you think I started and then even continued down this road with you? Do you doubt my sincerity?"

This interaction between them reminds Sarah of her final meeting with Hadassah – the way she aggressively reacted to Hadassah's insults. She struggled to maintain her professional veneer with Catherine, but her resolve had been weakened by those tenacious shadows that had been haunting her since she first took over Diane's group. She takes a breath and starts over by purposefully holding up a positive mirror for Catherine to view:

"I am a great admirer of yours, Catherine. I truly believe you will heal not only yourself, but your family as well. You are a fearless warrior when it comes to them — take pride in that. I also know that you have faith enough to change yourself in order to do what must be done. We will continue our work together to see this through. There will be setbacks — there are always — but as long as we anticipate them, we will find the tools to sail right by them."

Catherine's pent-up dam of tears breaks at Sarah's words. She just needed to hear those words from someone she had come to for validation…to adjust her self-image for her.

"Sarah, you cannot know how awful I feel about what I said to you about Hadassah…I know it was not your fault. Hadassah was a lost soul way before you came into the picture. I'm no therapist, but I blame her parents…"

Sarah cuts her short: "No blame in here, Catherine, especially not on people long gone. We must learn forgiveness and acceptance in here, which we can then bring with us to the outside world. Hadassah wasn't capable of those traits, but you are — release those past transgressions from your heart — your mother's, your daughter-in-law's and especially your own."

Catherine holds Sarah's hand and places it over her heart. "You get me, Sarah – you really get me."

After she leaves, Sarah muses on the past seven months:

It's really all a matter of perspective. Catherine and I are a team — we have the same goals so we must learn to work together to achieve them and not at cross purposes. This is not a competition. I can use that analogy with her for the next session — she and her daughter-in-law are on the same side, but Catherine needs to adjust the game plan to suit that of her teammate. If she thinks of it from that perspective, she will succeed along with her family. The picture may have changed, but she will grow to like it.

GEORGE

George is noticeably shaky when he enters the room; his body is trembling, his face is agitated, and his mouth is twitching. Sarah had never seen him like this…he usually presented himself with a steady demeanor. Even his clothing was disheveled: a stained shirt that was wrinkled and incorrectly buttoned, shoes that appeared to be bedroom slippers, and bleached-out work pants. George had not shaved for a few days, nor had he showered or ran a comb through his hair that morning. Sarah is disconcerted by his overall appearance and mannerisms; something is definitely amiss. Without wasting a minute, George begins berating himself:

"I am so unbelievably dumb...how could I not have seen this coming? He was always a problem — everyone knows that — but this! Oh, I'm an enabler alright, leaving them out like that — in full view, right where he could see them! Only I could make such a blunder...me, a silly, ridiculous, doddering old man whose judgement is so poor that he would put out a welcome mat for his own killer!"

He begins to cough uncontrollably...when the hacking subsides, George pulls and twists at his throat — a nervous habit that Sarah had noticed in earlier sessions. She had not been given the chance to speak yet, but now uses the lull to ask him to clarify:

"What has happened?"

"Sorry – I forgot to tell you before I came here today. I feel like a wall has collapsed and buried me and I had to save myself before it was too late."

"Please go on — why do you feel that way? Is it because of Hadassah or Stella?"

Now even this dear man is going to hit me squarely in the face with more accusations and incriminations. Go ahead – I'm getting used to being the fall guy..."

George looks confused, as if Sarah is speaking in an incomprehensible foreign language.

"Who? No, Sarah, you're not hearing me...What does Hadassah or Stella have to do with my son? Though, I should have listened to Stella – she knows my boy much better than I ever will! He is a sociopath, a pathological liar, and now a proven thief!"

Sarah is mystified — what had his son done now? Held up a bank? Headed up a Ponzi scheme? Stolen someone's identity to commit fraud? Her last guess is closest to the truth.

"Sarah, I still can't believe that my own son, who I admit is far from perfect, took my credit cards and ran them up to their limits — some as high as twenty-five thousand dollars apiece. What's worse is that I never suspected that he was the perpetrator. When the banks contacted me to determine if these unusually high charges were fraudulent, I confirmed that they had to be incorrect. Five Prada suits, Tom Ford sunglasses, Gucci loafers…all purchased at Saks, when my go-to store is Target or Kohls. The next transactions were even worse: cash advances totaling close to seventy-five thousand dollars, which were obtained through blatant forgeries. That figure closely matched the amount that my son had been hounding me for over the course of the last few weeks — another get-rich-quick scheme of his, much like the many I had underwritten in the past. This time though, I refused to give in — you see, I followed your lead — and this is the result. Now, I either have to accept these credit card charges and endanger our financial future, or tell the truth and consequentially send my son to prison. I am in a real conundrum here — damned if I do and damned if I don't!"

"How does your wife want to handle this?"

"She absolutely refuses to allow our son to be convicted of fraud and forgery at our hands. She says his life will be ruined and that he will turn into a life-long felon if we do this to him. I know she is right, but shouldn't he have to learn the hard way? Do I have no choice but to stall my retirement and die at my desk? My wife and I have made so many sacrifices — rarely going to restaurants except Friendly's or the neighborhood diner, taking inexpensive vacations like driving to Florida and staying with relatives a few years back, and buying most of our clothing at garage sales, thrift shops, or outlets. Now, my son steals the credit I have earned and accrued through the years to treat himself to three-thousand dollar suits and three hundred dollar meals at someplace called Boulud Sud, whatever that is! The injustice just infuriates me! I should have spent that money instead of saving it; now I have nothing to show for all the hard work and miserly practices except for a wastrel son in a fancy outfit, which will soon be replaced by an orange jumpsuit."

George starts sobbing as he angrily stomps around the room. His desperation is about to overpower him – Sarah's "fixer mechanism" kicks in.

"The situation is not as desperate as it seems. First, you cannot be the one who sends your son to jail…the guilt will destroy you. Instead, accept the charges and then work with the credit card companies to create a payment plan, which your son must contribute towards. I will see what I can do to reach out to my contacts; perhaps we can find him a steady income with one of them. Next, you, your wife, and your son should attend meetings that address the issues facing you all: for your son, his rampant spending sprees, his living well beyond his means while expecting others to foot the bill, and his total disregard for his lifetime of failure need to be analyzed by trained specialists in these matters. Once he acknowledges that he does in fact behave in ways that are destructive to both him and his family, he can begin to change in a positive way. Again, I stress the Golden Rule: watch out for yourself first before you try to improve the people around you!"

"That may work, but why do you want my wife and I to participate in meetings for over-spenders? We are the ants in this life fable and he is the grasshopper."

"I want you to attend Al-Anon, the group we spoke of at our first session. They are geared towards family members of addicts — drug addicts, alcoholics, and even shopaholics. You need to see that you are not alone in this predicament, but, more importantly, that you are not blameworthy for your son's mistakes and choices. George, remember that mirror I described back then — how my job was to show you how the world sees you?"

"Yes, but I kind of got lost in the storm. I know I have to stop giving in to my son's demands — this last episode has cured me of that impulse — but even after all this, I still feel as if I am abandoning him to a terrible fate. I am grateful for your proposal, but I don't know if he will keep his promises. Then, what do I do?"

"Don't worry about that — it is quite possible that he will not voluntarily contribute anything towards the debts he incurred, but legal arrangements can be made between his employer and you that would preclude that from happening. Those details can be worked out at another time. For now, you must surely recognize that you are not only a good father, but a moral man. Many others would have turned their backs on a son like yours, but you are not built like them. Your virtue makes you strong; it does not make you weak. You cannot bring yourself to condemn the boy, even though such an action would be accepted and expected in our society. We hear about "tough love" and "boot camps" as ways to scare our misguided children onto a new road, but here you are — taking a stand against such methods — why? ...Because you love your son and have faith that your love will be enough to guide him through. Perspective changes things, you know. You may be seeing things one way, and I see them in another – So, look in my mirror, George – be proud of who you are and accept my vision of you because, in the end, it's your self-perception that truly matters."

He looks into Sarah's eyes in order to find his reflection there. He sits back in his chair, deep in thought. After a minute or so, George runs his hands through his unkempt hair, adjusts his shirt, and brushes off his trousers. The tremors have dissipated and his mouth is much more relaxed. He has a determined look — unlike the old George, who looked nonchalant and carefree, but who was clearly hiding something beneath the surface.

"Sarah, I wasn't going to come here today. I had totally lost all hope, but my instincts pushed me out of my stupor and prodded me to get going to see you. I am glad I did. I am beginning to understand what's here inside of me, and I like it. You did that for me — as you said, you changed my perspective. It's a whole new notion, and it will take more work with you, but I can honestly say that I can feel the old me fading — turning into a shadow, I guess is how I would describe it. Its outline is still there, but the substance is just a hazy blur. Am I making any sense to you?"

More than you know, dear George...

"I am looking forward to our future sessions together. You are on your way now — and you will not be turning back! I will be in touch with you about your son very soon."

As George leaves, Sarah can hear him whistling a tune she knows, but could not place in her head — it was jaunty and lively — a good omen for both of them.

SARAH

As she methodically reviewed her notes on both the group and individual sessions over the past seven months, Sarah realized that she had omitted the parts that pertained to her: the visions — the memories — the fantasies — that each of these patients had stirred up in her, beginning with Stella. She knew that these phantoms were an integral part of her work with these patients, and she worried that her reactions had distorted her perceptions. Sarah had even questioned her reasons for choosing her life's work during one of her sessions with George...this group of patients had come within striking distance of destroying Sarah, but from whose perspective was she judging the final decision? Unable to answer this question definitively, she shuffled the note packets as in any game of chance. As Fate would have it, the folder that landed on top was none other than her nemesis – Stella.

Stella had knowingly played with her; she was acutely aware of her power over Sarah and used it to her best advantage, but had Stella really gotten the upper hand? When she reread her notes, Sarah saw that she had made progress with this patient, admittedly impossible to discern with the naked eye, but as a deeply intuitive therapist, Sarah could see beyond Stella's subterfuge…at least it seemed that way to her.

Oh how I long to escape from this hall of mirrors! The fun house is no longer any fun — it just mixes me up…what's up is down and what's down is up. Am I really attracted to Stella and is she actually flirting with me, or is that just my devious side playing havoc with my senses again? Sarah, you've been a naughty girl — but you are not completely lost. Follow your advice — face the mirrors with courage and self-conviction — they're the only way to salvation!

She feared what her introspection would uncover. Her hand rested upon the file beneath Stella's – Paul! Sarah shuddered…not only with a sharp foreboding, but also with an undeniable passion. Now here was a case in which her defense was at its weakest. She wanted Paul; she longed for his touch and his love.

I even encouraged him to try making love to a woman…when I knew beyond the shadow of a doubt that such an undertaking would only con-fuse him! From the start, I erected obstacles to Paul's embracing of his homosexuality …paying no attention to his outburst in our first group meeting. Was I drawn to him that early on? No, I was merely setting parameters that needed to be set from the get-go – I am sure of that. My nature is just too controlling to allow any wiggle room…but still, those steamy sex scenes I played over and over again in my head! Am I really that lonely?

Shaking off her last notion, Sarah is pleased to find Barry and Gladys next — now here, at least, was one success story. Gladys glowed from within and Barry seemed much more comfortable as the dominant partner. Sarah also found satisfaction in his new-found skill of mentalization; in fact, Barry, of all people, was her star pupil! Not only did he anticipate and satisfy his wife's needs, but he also was more proficient in understanding the rest of the group, including Sarah herself.

But was I also feeling a vicarious thrill as I listened to their sexual play-by-plays? Their fantasies certainly aroused my more salacious memories of Walter…were my sessions with them simply pornographic exercises? Sarah, stop accusing yourself of behaving so horribly…once again, it's that persistent guilt spawned by your mother that threatens to overpower you. Where did the new Sarah disappear to and why?

Catherine's frowning folder taunted Sarah as it sat waiting impatiently to be read. She and Catherine had much in common, but Sarah had consciously chosen not to divulge all that much of herself to this patient, fearing her disappointment as well as her perceptive judgment. While she was confident that she had guided Catherine to the point at which she would be willing to change her perspective towards her daughter-in-law, would Sarah feel at ease confessing her own crushing weaknesses to Catherine going forward?

From the start, Catherine challenged my self-assurance…seeing my inner doubts and fears with a clarity that was disquieting. Apart from Stella, Catherine rattled me far more than any of the others and I am certain that she was aware of her effect on me. Yet, she chose to scuttle it — never taking advantage of her secret weapon to gain the upper hand. She is a Giver alright! I believe she felt that I deserved that chance — in the years to come, that thought will sustain me.

Sarah's self-evaluations were suddenly shaded in optimism, which increased when she saw George's name as the next-in-line. That last session was a turning point for him, and, with Sarah's help, he had made it to the other side despite the dark forces that had placed him in such danger.

In spite of the fact that it was George who innocently derailed me when I discussed recreating his image…holding up a positive mirror to help him dispel the negative perceptions instilled in him by his parents…I still trusted enough in my skills as a therapist to proceed with my advice — and it was the right decision! No second-guessing my intentions this time…but, what about my original reasons for becoming a therapist all those years ago? I claim to have sought peace for my troubled family. When I failed, I chose my field so that I could at least succeed with other tormented souls. I still can see my mother lying prostrate on the floor… fooled into believing she was the one in control of the family — while I manipulated all of them in order to possess my father, body and soul.

Sarah turned away from a scene she thought had been annihilated into ashes through therapy, but the branding was all too strong — the therapeutic blister reopened. She was in agony; she grasped Pauline's packet, in search of its promise of a soothing balm within its pages. Perusing her notes, Sarah was gratified of the reminder that her personal experience had served as a beacon of hope to her flailing and wavering patient. In this case, Sarah was comfortable enough to face the mirror and there she saw herself as a selfless and compassionate therapist. She begins to feel her angst disappearing, but then…

My success with Pauline validates me…why didn't her outcome extend to the rest of the group? Is it because my experience so closely shadowed hers? Perhaps, I am not the genius I think I am…not a full-fledged member of the illuminati. Someone recently described me as feeling "superior," but who?

A wretched face swims up from the depths of her musings – Hadassah! Sarah curses at her as if she were the devil itself. She looks down at the note packets — not one remained. She searches for the file on Hadassah, momentarily forgetting that she had buried it in a remote desk drawer. She had never wanted to look at it again…the word "SUICIDE" stamped in red across the front of the folder…but now she is frantic to find it, throwing aside piles of notes that had been haphazardly, yet logically organized in piles by color — a system Sarah had developed and utilized over her years as a therapist: Pinks for the Abuse Victims, Reds for the Anger Bordering on Psychotic Patients, Blues for the Depressed People, Gray for the Borderlines, etc. She had not even bothered to assign a color to Hadassah – which spoke to her perplexity as well as her active dislike for this woman. The white folder somehow found its way into her hands.

Here it is…why is it white??? – Even in death, Hadassah irritates me. What didn't I see and why didn't I see what was going on inside of her? She was closed…so why didn't I at least try to crack open her door? I know Hadassah's view of me matched my own impressions completely…I had been sailing blithely through life, which I now see would eventually have damaged me beyond repair. Maybe she unknowingly did me a favor?

Sarah had achieved catharsis — she took the next step by scheduling an appointment to re-enter a round of therapy, feeling much better enlightened about herself than she had all the times prior to this shadowy journey. Yes, the shades still frightened her — those misty wisps in their gloomy aspects with their doomsday prophecies — but Sarah had companions this time around. The parade of pilgrims passes before Sarah: Stella the Sinner… Barry and Gladys, the Married Couple…Pauline, the Lady-in-Waiting…Catherine, the Meddler… Paul, the Knight-in-Arms… George, the Fixer…Hadassah, the Wretch…and finally Sarah herself…the Lost Pilgrim. Each of them had had a profound influence on Sarah's perspective on the world and her place within it. She had been twisted around by them in so many ways that she was now feeling that her life was suddenly topsy-turvy, but she had also evolved into a woman who accepted her limitations, yet was still brave enough to face this new world standing on her head.

EPILOGUE

It has been almost a year since we left our pilgrims mid-journey, so to speak. The original group has continued to meet as before, but some have ended their weekly individual sessions with Sarah, changing the schedule to an "as needed" basis. Each of them has continued to thrive, with some leading the way for the rest of the group.

Stella the Sinner – She has been meeting with Sarah in individual sessions on a bi-weekly basis (although, at first, the sessions took place weekly at Sarah's request). Stella has separated from her husband until she is more adept at recognizing how her behavior is actually prompting the abuse. She remains at odds with Sarah by tempting her to inflict more damage upon both of them, but Sarah's resistance has proven to be more formidable now. To satisfy her curiosity, Stella had a dalliance with a lesbian lover, but it went nowhere due to Stella's insincerity. Lately, she has become more focused on her marriage and continues to work diligently to reconcile with her husband. She is even considering couples' therapy as an option – with Sarah, of course.

Barry and Gladys: The Married Couple – Their sex life continues to improve since Barry never returned to his original passivity. With him in the driver's seat, Gladys no longer feels the need to be in control, which means that Barry now takes responsibility for his own actions. He is more attentive to the needs of his wife and children, making him happier than he has ever been in his life. He continues to attend group sessions, but he and Gladys only come to Sarah as a couple when they have to attend an upcoming family get-together, an event which both expect may lead to a familiar disagreement…so they take preventive action.

Pauline the Lady-in-Waiting – She now has what she has wanted for so long – a baby girl born through surrogacy. Since the baby takes up most of her time, Pauline has left the group and no longer has individual sessions with Sarah. However, she does call Sarah with questions on how to deal with questions and reactions from her friends and family. Since she was honest with them from the start regarding the surrogacy, they often pose questions to Pauline about her baby's origins – and her feelings towards the baby. She fears that her self-doubts will re-emerge and so she speaks to Sarah at length, more as her friend than as her therapist. Sarah continues to assure her that she is indeed the true mother and Pauline has come to take on that role with growing confidence.

Catherine the Meddler – As Sarah began to confide in Catherine, her words of advice took on a more pertinent meaning. Seeing that Sarah realized that she had to help herself before being able to help her patient gave Catherine the insight she needed to relinquish control over her daughter-in-law and her family. Now, Catherine is making a conscious effort to change her preconceived ideas about the situation and the results show. Her daughter-in-law is considering joining a group that Sarah recommended to Catherine. Once Catherine listened to the needs of her whole family, without judgement, criticism, or advice, they were more willing to listen to her. It is still a work-in-progress, but Catherine's baby steps have proven to be more effective that her customary leaps and bounds.

Paul the Knight-in-Arms – Once Sarah ceased having fantasies about him, she was able to encourage him to welcome his sexual identity with open arms. At that point, Paul married his gay lover, which gave him the stability he needed to forego individual therapy. In group, Paul continues to serve as Sarah's helpmate when needed, which has made the group more and more cohesive. His overall outlook inspires the rest of them to take heart in their own futures.

George the Fixer – Taking Sarah's advice, George was able to develop a working payment plan for his son to reimburse him for the monies he had stolen. When his son saw that George was no longer a push-over, he developed a long overdue respect for his father who had now found a way to partially dispel those feelings of guilt that had eaten at him for most of his life. George attends both group and individual sessions with Sarah to secure his newly formed character that still feels strange to him.

Hadassah the Wretch – Through her self-sacrifice, Hadassah saved Sarah. She continues to burn brightly in Sarah's heart – no longer a figure of despair, but rather an avenging spirit who came to shepherd Sarah out of the shadows.

Sarah the Lost Pilgrim – She continues to participate in individual therapy as well as in a group, which she formed for therapists who had lost patients to suicide. No longer isolated from her peers, her friends, and her patients, Sarah carries on in her quest for answers.

The shadows that are shadowing me hold the key – much like Hadassah. Open your eyes, Sarah and be not afraid of what they reveal to you. Your salvation awaits you, dear pilgrim…

www.ingramcontent.com/pod-product-compliance
Lightning Source LLC
Chambersburg PA
CBHW070805240726

48654CB00007B/213